REMEMBERED

SKY

CHARLIE COMINS

To Miranda
Enjoy the read.
Kate
x

Published by New Generation Publishing in 2020

Copyright © Charlotte (Charlie) Comins 2020

First Edition

The author asserts the moral right under the Copyright, Designs and Patents Act 1988 to be identified as the author of this work.

All Rights reserved. No part of this publication may be reproduced, stored in a retrieval system or transmitted, in any form or by any means without the prior consent of the author, nor be otherwise circulated in any form of binding or cover other than that which it is published and without a similar condition being imposed on the subsequent purchaser.

ISBN: 978-1-78955-860-9

www.newgeneration-publishing.com

New Generation Publishing

Disclaimer:

This is primarily a book of memory and memory has its own story to tell. It reflects the author's experience of a particular time and place in the past; some names and characteristics have been changed, some events have been compressed and some dialogue has been recreated. The author has sought and been given permission to include the memories of others in this work.

Website: www.ccomins-blueskybook.com

In my chest are two holes, shot there by the gentle-eyed sheriff
My blood gushed instantly from those two escape routes
I knew my blood was going home, and me along with it
Above me is my only enemy – the dry blue sky
It has consumed me totally while running, shooting, even making love
But the only time it fails to consume me is when I die
Now I will not be consumed
For the first time I have no fear of the blue sky
I am not afraid of that silence, that fathomless blue
I can go home now to where I don't have to fight

Shuntaro Tanikawa – Billy the Kid

Background

Southern Rhodesia was a self-governing British colony in Africa. The colony was established in 1923, having previously been administered by the British South Africa Company. In 1953 Southern Rhodesia merged into a Federation with Northern Rhodesia (now Zambia) and Nyasaland (now Malawi). The Federation ended in 1963 when the latter two countries achieved independence. In 1965 the white-supremacist government of Ian Douglas Smith issued a Unilateral Declaration of Independence (UDI) from Great Britain and Rhodesia became an un-recognised state. A brutal liberation struggle followed, known as the Second Chimurenga by the indigenous population, and as the Rhodesian war by the white minority. In 1979 peace was brokered and on 17th April 1980, Robert Mugabe was elected as the Prime Minister of Zimbabwe.

The Ingutsheni Lunatic Asylum was built in 1908 and was one of the largest such institutions of its kind, eventually receiving 'mad people' from all three countries in the Federation. In 1930, England and Wales passed the Mental Treatment Act and the asylum became a mental hospital in 1933. The first trained alienist (psychiatrist) ever employed in the colony, Dr. Kenneth Mann Rodger, became the medical superintendent of Ingutsheni in October 1933. In 1936 Southern Rhodesia's Legislative Council passed the Mental Disorders Act. The 1936 law established a Mental Hospitals Board composed of prominent members of the white community. They tended to defer to Rodger's judgment because he was a highly respected specialist.

Charlotte Comins and her family lived in the grounds of Ingutsheni from 1956-1971. For most of her life she kept her past a secret. When she began to explore her childhood memories and the moral, political and economic world in which she grew up, a troubling story emerged.

I have now come to know that what one believes can often become permanent, and what becomes permanent can be indestructible.

Chigozie Obioma

Our language is an imperfect instrument created by ancient and ignorant men. It is an animistic language that invites us to talk about stability and constants, about similarities, normal and kinds, about magical transformations, quick cures, simple problems and final solutions. Yet the world we try to symbolise with this language is a world of process, change, differences, dimensions, functions, relationships, growths, interactions, developing, learning, coping, complexity.

Marshall Rosenberg quoting Wendell Johnson

Each of us is more than the worst thing we have ever done.

Kirsty Young introducing Bryan Stevenson, an American human rights lawyer on Desert Island Discs, BBC Radio 4, 8 March 2015

For my family

The aim of therapy is not to correct the past, but to enable the patient to confront his own history, and to grieve over it.

Alice Miller

This book is dedicated to people affected by psychiatric labels, treatment, medication and stigma

The first recorded lunatic asylum in Europe was the Bethlem Royal Hospital in London.

It has been part of London since 1247 when it was built as a priory.

It became a hospital in 1330 and admitted its first mentally ill patients in 1407.

Before the Madhouse Act of 1774, treatment of the insane was carried out by non-licensed practitioners who ran their madhouses as a commercial enterprise with little regard for the inmates.

Wikipedia

The disease theory of schizophrenia treats these structures as no more than symptoms of the illness and not as being meaningful in themselves. Over the past forty years I have been told, time and time again, that scientists are on the verge of discovering the physiological cause of schizophrenia.

Forty years is a very long time to be on the verge.

Dorothy Rowe

Women were locked up for having even mild post-natal depression: the grandmother of a friend of mine spent her life in an asylum after throwing a scourer at her mother-in-law. At least one US psychiatric text book, still widely in use in the 1970s recommended lobotomies for women in abusive relationships.

Are anti-depressants the new (and obviously preferable) lobotomy for women dealing with trauma?

Caroline Criado Perez

'Borderline personality disorder' reflects the assumption that the individual is damaged and bad.

Whatever an individual has suffered – rape, abuse, homophobia, poverty – the linguistic category of 'BPD' states that the cause of their distress exists within them. The individual - rather than the traumatic experience, the family, the society – becomes the problem. Coping strategies, ingenuity, courage, the drive to survive are reframed in the language of 'disorder'.

Clare Shaw

Psychiatric diagnosis is the first cause of everything bad that happens in the mental health system, because if they don't diagnose you, they cannot do *anything* to you, but once they give you *any* of the hundreds of diagnoses, they can do pretty much anything to you in the name of treatment. And, because psychiatric diagnosis is totally unregulated, there is no oversight and little or no recourse for those who are harmed. The harm ranges from loss of self-confidence to loss of physical health, employment, child custody and the right to make decisions about one's medical and legal affairs – even to loss of life.

Paula J. Caplan

The Power Threat Meaning Framework patterns are based on the evidence that people construct typical meanings in response to certain kinds of threat, such as feeling excluded, rejected, trapped, coerced or shamed, and may respond in characteristic ways. Thus, the patterns describe what people **do**, not illnesses they **have**. This is summarised in the phrase *patterns of embodied, meaning-based responses to threat*. It may be useful to draw on these patterns to help develop people's personal stories, and to convey a message of acceptance and validation, such as people sometimes find in diagnosis from knowing that they are not alone in their struggles.

Lucy Johnstone

Foreword

I am very pleased to introduce this remarkable book. Part history, part autobiography, it takes us on a journey through the author's childhood, growing up next to a psychiatric hospital where her formidable father was a psychiatrist, in what was then Rhodesia (now Zimbabwe). There were happy times playing with the family's servants and running wild in the bushland with a freedom unknown to children today. But everything was overshadowed by her father's harshness and rages, and the haunted figures that could be glimpsed or heard behind the walls of the hospital grounds. British colonialism and the struggle for liberation formed the background to her childhood. Charlie's family were members of the white minority, and yet their lives too were touched by violence in many forms.

The narrative includes some of Charlie's visits to her therapist, whom she sought out after her life started unravelling in her mid-fifties. After much detective work and agonising self-reflection, Charlie's father's secret history emerges, along with heartrending details about her mother, throwing light on Charlie's own struggles. All of their stories are intertwined with the bigger narrative of the colonial regime which imported Western psychiatry as one of its tools of domination. Charlie was unknowingly brought up in the shadow of ruthless brutality inflicted on members of the indigenous population who had been deemed 'mad.' Her father's job was to perpetuate this process in the name of psychiatry.

This is a profoundly thought-provoking book about trauma, oppression and domination, but also, ultimately, about truth-seeking, healing and freedom.

Lucy Johnstone

Lead author with Professor Mary Boyle of the Power Threat Meaning Framework (PTMF) in collaboration with service users, people who work in mental health and other members of the helping professions

Prologue

I remember the first time I drove over to Sandi's house; how being welcomed into her front room with its soft, pearly-grey walls and carved wooden piano did little to soothe my nerves. I remember how I tentatively sat myself down on a comfortable cream sofa facing a wide bay window. The sun was shining behind some white curtains and I could just make out the faint grey shapes of tiny birds printed on the fabric. Sandi seated herself opposite me in a tan-coloured armchair. The brass studs on the chair's upholstery made it appear somewhat exotic as if it came from another world. Her bold flowery skirt, ample bosom and beaming smile made me feel encouraged that I was in the company of someone who was keen to get to know more about me, and who wanted to put me at my ease as best she could. "Welcome, Charlie," she said. "You could start by telling me a little bit about your background if you like."

I like the way Sandi speaks and also her relaxed posture. It takes away some of my unease at the novelty of talking about myself to a complete stranger. I giggle nervously as I make a start.

"Men didn't call us girls 'girls' when I was growing up. My older sister Elaine was 'a brainy bird' and Justine was a 'party bird'. Justine was a bit of a celebrity because she was so stunningly beautiful. I'm not sure what kind of 'bird' exactly I was supposed to be but I remember feeling happy when a friend of my mother's said I had a great looking pair of legs." I laugh. "Also, I remember Yael said I was 'some chick' when I plastered myself with make-up and wore my pink hot pants outfit. My father ... he called me 'little miss pussy' because I fussed over a litter of kittens belonging to a feral cat who lived in our garage.

Mother Pussy was a tabby cat. She had made a sort of cat nest in amongst some old hessian sacks in the darkest corner of the garage. I can still remember what a joy it was to have those kittens to watch and pet as they got bigger." Suddenly something huge and dark and foreboding makes its presence felt and stops me in my tracks. I try to gather my thoughts and I feel slightly at sea as if I'm going to float away. Sandi doesn't say anything. She just sits quietly with an enquiring look on her face but my lost thread eludes me. The bright sunlight outside her window beams through my shimmering memories like a long-lost and much needed friend.

"It's the words ... you see, the words people used were all very de-humanising at that time ... in ... in that place. Even ... even at the hospital, the women's ward had an outdoor exercise yard which was enclosed by iron railings that were shaped like flamingos, but they were really strange-looking birds with elongated legs and necks, big hooked beaks and empty circular wings. Perhaps the authorities thought that all women are just silly bird brains or sex kittens ...."

I remember the pained expression on Sandi's face as she listened, and I remember that it felt unbelievably good to be shown such obvious interest and concern.

I barrel on feeling slightly reassured.
"I don't know anything about my father except that he was born in Cape Town and that he was Jewish. Elaine and Justine were born in London a few years before my parents emigrated to Rhodesia. I grew up in such a beautiful country, you know ... there were amazing butterflies, jacaranda and flamboyant trees ... and we went for picnics in the Matopos where I climbed up mountains made of boulders. I saw rock paintings that had been there for thousands of years, and we watched antelope, and giraffes, and zebras grazing ... I ... I hardly ever wore shoes ... At the hospital we had night apes living

Prologue

in our roof and I followed guinea fowl roaming around in the long grass near our house. The bauhinia tree near my bedroom was covered in lilac and white flowers and I used to love watching the tiny sunbirds that came to feed in amongst all the pretty flowers ..."

Sandi shifts in her chair and I remember that I'm here to talk about myself. "I ... I feel English in so many ways but I'm not really because I was born in Africa. I can't tell you how I've longed to be an African. I used to wish I was black, you know. I can't stand it when people say that I'm an old colonial or that I'm a Rhodesian. I ... I've lived in England now for more than half my life and I still don't know who I am or where I belong." I laugh a bit too loudly. "I'm going to be an interesting case ... nutcase, I mean! My father thought I was ... well, he said I'm immature ... and ... and unrealistic, deluded ... and self-deceptive ... I'm ... I'm not even sure that I'm intelligent enough to be here ..."

"Well, he was your father. So, you would have believed him," Sandi says.

For a moment her words took my breath away. The bright sunshine outside the window turned her curtains into a big white sky where freedom and possibility greeted me unexpectedly. I remember how I sat and gazed at the little grey birds flying randomly on Sandi's curtains and suddenly I knew that I could tell her things I'd never wanted to think about, let alone talk about openly to anyone before.

Blue Remembered Sky

PART ONE

The Hospital

The oft-quoted 'one in four' statistic relating to incidence of mental 'illness' neatly separates a quarter of the population from the other three-quarters. This perception of 'them and us' leads to the belief that there are people we, as counsellors, can work with, and those we cannot.

Yet none of us is immune to the emotional toll of adversity, abuse, trauma, loss and discrimination. All of us strive to feel safe and to avoid pain and distress.

We need to explicitly challenge 'them and us', 'one in four' and 'diagnosis and disorder' in order to empower our students to be able to see past such unhelpful labels.

Jenny Taper and Jamie-Lee Tipping

We still live in a world in which, you know, the male norm is the default and in which the girl is still slightly 'the other'. And there are so many brilliant people who are changing that but we inherited two thousand years of misogyny and it hasn't gone away yet.

Katherine Rundell, BBC Radio 4,
"The Everywoman" - 2 June 2020

Blue Remembered Sky

One

My mother Susan was a beautiful woman. Her deep blue eyes were framed by sweeping eyebrows. She was blessed with lovely high cheekbones and a sensual smile. She had a distinctive, somewhat husky voice and thick wavy brown hair. She could easily have been Ingrid Bergman's sister.

Susan had been a nurse when she met Lionel some time during World War Two. Her early promise as a ballet dancer was evident in her elegant posture and the beautifully cut dresses with matching accessories that she chose with such care. She loved Italian shoes and handbags because she said they were made by master craftsmen, worth every penny she spent on them. When I turned eighteen, she took me to Ramji and Sons, an upmarket clothing store, and bought me a beige suede coat. I was wearing it when I met Gordon. He came to visit me and met my family in 1976 when we'd been living in suburbia for nearly five years. I'm sure he took in my fashionable outfits, our elegant home with its Persian rugs and antique furniture, our swimming pool that sparkled in the sunshine, the pale green Citroen shaped like a frog in the carport, and decided my family was wealthy and cultured beyond his wildest dreams. I know I thought we were.

My mother would gracefully do the splits when asked to do so, even though her joints made clicking noises as she lowered herself to the floor. She used to remind me that she won the hurdles at her sports days when she was at secondary school. She got a scholarship to attend a grammar school but going to university wasn't readily encouraged in 1937. The only time I saw her cry was when

I quit my studies at the University of Cape Town to go and do a secretarial course.

My father Lionel bore a vague resemblance to the actor David Niven in the photograph I have of him as a young man. Yael said Lionel's huge collection of silk ties were given to him by grateful patients. My father always wore a tie with one of his muted grey or cream-coloured shirts. In the winter he donned a pale-blue cashmere cardigan that he bought from Eric Davis, a men's outfitter in the centre of town. My mother admired his taste in jackets with their walnut buttons and soft woollen weave; she loved his charcoal silk suit best, with its fine grey stripes. He came home with it after a visit to McCullogh and Bothwell, a shop for men with discerning taste and an income to match. His dark brown Hush Puppy shoes were his trademark, along with his Rotary Club cufflinks and his Marriage Guidance Council tie pin.

I've only got three photos of Lionel Perelman before he became my father. One is an official portrait of him wearing his Medical Officer's uniform during the war, from which I've studied his twinkling eyes and neatly clipped moustache at least a million times. I would study my own face in the mirror as I grew older, alarmed to see that it resembled my father's face quite strongly. It made me long to be as beautiful as Elaine and Justine. It didn't help that my mother insisted on cropping my hair as short as a boy's. I spent my childhood lusting after my sisters' long plaits, fashionable fringes and pointy nails. My nails were bitten so badly that I hid them away in my pockets.

My father kept his hands carefully manicured and his hair bryl-creamed into place. His speech was sprinkled with Afrikaans words like 'hekkies' for pimples and 'guti' for the damp mist that shrouded the trees on cold winter days. Lionel liked to laugh at his own jokes, especially the names he came up with for people he disliked, or even people he liked. Maybe that's how doctors and nurses keep themselves smiling. His favourite hobby was cleaning the nicotine out of his cigarette holder with a pipe cleaner. I always gave him pipe cleaners for his birthday because that's what my mother said he liked best. He cleaned her cigarette holder at the same time as he cleaned his, so perhaps she had a vested interest in keeping him well supplied. His Old Spice Aftershave and the Sea and Ski cream he used for sunbathing gave him a familiar sweet smell.

My parents shared gossip at mealtimes about their medical friends and the goings-on at the hospital. When I was older, I used to ask my father how his day had been. He'd shake his head and say, "Things are bad chum." Or else he'd say, "No news is good news." I would nod enthusiastically even though I hadn't a clue what he was talking about. It was the same when he shook his head and said, "One must never speak ill of the dead." He didn't talk about people who were dead, so his comment made little sense to me.

On Sundays our servants had the day off and my mother would make us a roast with all the trimmings for lunch. At the end of the meal, my father would throw his napkin onto the table next to his empty plate and say "That was excellent Susie. Are you sure it wasn't Anderson who made it?" My mother would click her tongue and look annoyed. My father was the only person who was allowed to call her Susie; she was very particular about names. She asked my friend Shareen to stop calling me Charlie. She didn't care that I was being gangster when Shareen called me Bugsy. She said nicknames were for pets, not people.

It was impossible to be a person of any note in my father's world unless you were a fellow doctor. Susan, being a nurse, was on a par with our servants. He regarded his wife, and us girls as irrational, wayward creatures. We were expected to listen to what he said, for his knowledge in all things was superior to ours. My mother was thrilled that he gave her free access to his earnings so that she could run his life with taste and finesse. She set about creating a home and life-style equivalent to the British aristocracy, so I guess she felt more than compensated when he spoke to her like he did. Lionel liked fancy cars, a stiff whisky in the evenings and time to listen to sport on his portable radio. He loved the Citroen that he bought for my mother because it was the same pale green as the Studebaker he'd owned when he was a newly qualified doctor.

When I was born, Lionel apparently took one look at me in the hospital and said "Ah, sweet Charlotte. We can call her Charlie can't we Susie?" My birth, three years after my family set sail for Rhodesia, confirmed my parents' commitment to stay and work for the British colonial government in Southern Rhodesia. Once three years were up, the cost of their passage was waived. When I was a year old, my father was given free accommodation in the hospital grounds, and we moved into a bungalow over the road from the women's ward.

In April 1957, my younger brother Yael was born. For the next sixteen years, until our father retired from government service, the hospital and the vast bushland around it was the place that we called home.

Two

When Yael was a little baby, he nearly died. My mother wrote: *"You were twenty months old when Yael was born. I gave him very small amounts of 'Farex' from age approximately three weeks, then he was happy and full, and he began to sleep well. He, I wonder if you remember, was very ill with pneumonia when he was ten months old. He was already walking but still partially breast-fed. He was taken into the Mater Dei Hospital and abruptly weaned in an oxygen tent and literally, almost died. Neville Saunders found a new antibiotic that had just been introduced on the market and tried it on this poor child, who remarkably, benefitted from it, and made a very smooth recovery although it was noticeable that he had suffered emotionally from being 'snatched' into the Mater Dei. He was very 'clingy' to me for some weeks and I suspect his tendency to 'dither' stems from that unsettled period in his early life. You probably suffered too, for all my focus at that time was on him and you were 'of moment'. You were very healthy, and Mary did a lot of looking after you when I was visiting Yael. Perhaps that's what made you jealous of him. You were approximately two and a half years old and had never shown up to then, nor after so far as I know, any overt signs of jealousy. You never hit him, pinched, bit or punched him, you just 'bossed' him around."*

Mary looked after Yael when he came home. She talked in a loud voice and when she smiled her teeth shone as white as icing sugar. She carried Yael around on her hip and sang him songs. She smelled different to my mother because her smokiness didn't have anything to do with cigarettes. I used to sit on the ground next to her so I could watch her light the fire and start cooking. In an iron pot, she made a meat stew from the rations my mother gave her. She made sadza by pounding dried mealies (maize or sweetcorn) into a flour. She added water until she'd created a thick paste. I watched her form the sadza into balls to dip into the rich brown stew. She boiled water in an iron kettle on the fire. I'd wait patiently for her to give me some of the stale bread she dipped into her dented mug. It was warm, sweet and tinny.

I used to creep into Mary's dark room behind the garage. There were no windows and it had a smooth dirt floor. It was like being in a cave until my eyes got used to being out of the sun. The floor was cool and pleasant on the soles of my bare feet. In the middle of the room was the open fire with its metal grid. Mary's sleeping mat was against the back wall.

Mary brought her baby to live with her in the shack for a while. She tied the baby onto her back with an old blanket, so all you could see was its fuzzy head lolling to one side as she bent over to pick Yael up or to sweep the floor.

One day I crept into Mary's room and found her baby sitting all by itself. The baby looked at me with its brown eyes. Snot streamed out of its nose and it didn't seem to mind the flies that buzzed in and out of it. I rushed over at the baby and gave it a hard push, so it flew over backwards with a thud. I ran back into the house and hid underneath my eiderdown. My ears tingled as I lay there and listened to the baby screaming. I stayed where I was for a long time afterwards.

My mother said Mary's husband was a boozer. One night, he and Mary had a fight. My mother laughed heartily when she told her friends what happened. "She just picked up the nearest thing to hand, hit him on the head with one LP after the other, and told him to get out!" Yael said Lionel gave Mary the sack after that. Elaine said Mary left because she wasn't allowed to stay long-term on our property with a baby. Margaret, our next nanny was older than Mary and although she didn't sing to us, I remember her as a kind and gentle soul.

I also have fond memories of Anderson who was our cook. In the only photograph I have of him, his outfit looks dazzling white in the bright sun. He used to sit in the shade under the palm tree, holding a round mirror in one hand and combing his wiry hair into a wide parting down the middle of his head. He had a neat moustache and his broad smile revealed a large gap between his front teeth. My mother taught him how to make Yorkshire puddings and roast beef. The only thing Anderson never learned to do was bake. My mother was a master chef when it came to making cakes. All my friends remember the chocolate cakes she made for my school tennis matches. Her butter cream chocolate icing was delicious. She whizzed a fork across the icing and turned it into wavy patterns like the choppy water of the sea. She scattered tiny silver balls liberally on top, like little pearls of wisdom, and perhaps a warning not to eat more than one piece of cake at a time.

Justine remembers Anderson's kindness: *"Don't know which was worse, being told by Mum that 'Dad will deal with you when he gets home' or Dad 'dealing with me!!!' Do you recall the time I went to the circus without permission? God, you would have thought the world ended. I got a 'hiding' and wasn't allowed to go anywhere for ages. But Anderson made up for it by making me a nice plate of sausages and tomato sauce to console me. I remember Dad once hit Elaine so hard he actually lifted her off her little feet. God knows what the poor little thing had done – she was always smaller than me in my mind. I think he once told me it was good discipline but he didn't hit any of us once we got into our teens. Probably today he would be considered an abusive father. I know that my friend's mother gave her children the odd smack. But nothing as violent as we had to go through. The strange part of it was it was mostly initiated by Mum. We certainly did have a strange childhood – wandering around the countryside alone at very young ages, walking alone to see friends in Hillside and the extremely strange belief that at five o'clock each day, any friends who had come over had to go home and the house had to be perfect so when Dad came home all was 'in order'."*

It was Anderson who came to the rescue when one of us woke in the morning to see the black shape of a rain spider on the mosquito net. He was sent along with a broom stick to hit the spider off the net. I waited, shivering under my sheet, while he clubbed it to death on our floor. Rain spiders were commonplace in the summer months, when rain deluged our garden and turned it into an insect-loving swamp.

In the afternoons, a thunderstorm brought relief from the blazing heat. The servants rushed outside in excitement, wielding kitchen sieves to scoop up squirming heaps of flying ants to add to their stews. They also roasted locusts, mealies and fat mopani worms on the fire. It made no difference that we couldn't understand a word they were saying for they never shooed us away. I squatted on the floor next to them, ate what they offered me and breathed in their smells and the loudness of their chatter. Our servants epitomised life for me. Their bodies shook when they laughed, and their hands slapped together when they said hello and goodbye. They sucked air in between their front teeth and laughed when they talked. We copied Anderson when he shouted 'haikorna' as a word of warning. Margaret blew on Yael's knees when they were bleeding and I sat in the warmth of her lap when something upset me. She clicked her tongue and said, "shame shame" and "agh agh" until I stopped crying. I remember how Margaret once put Yael's foot up to her mouth so she could pull out a sharp thorn with her teeth.

She taught me to trail a tiny stick around the rim of an ant bear hole. This made the occupant shoot upwards in a shower of sand. I spent hours trailing a twig around the tops of sandy holes, waiting for an ant bear to pounce. When an ant fell in, I watched it disappear in a puff of sand.

Three

Winifred Davies was the occupational therapist at the hospital. She dropped by for a cup of tea at our house after work most afternoons. She and my parents would sit outdoors underneath the thatched shelter smoking their cigarettes. We children played nearby while the servants came and went with pots of tea, or glasses chinking with ice cubes. In the winter, they sat in the lounge and we were invited in to say a brief "Hallo". I watched my mother pluck ice out of a sweating silver bucket with a pair of tongs. She dropped blocks of ice into their drinks with a crack while their cigarettes made smoky trails around their heads. Winifred, with her blonde bob and pointy shoes, had a clipped way of speaking and a shrieky laugh. She didn't have a deep voice like my mother, nor did she have my mother's musical way of petting the bulldog, which often came and snuffled under her skirt.

Years later, when I was expecting my first child, I got in touch with Winifred who was living in Colchester. She sent me a cassette recording of her memories of working at the hospital. She described how, in 1952, she'd decided to apply for a job abroad after a pea-soup fog stopped all the buses on her way to work one cold winter morning in London. She felt it would do her good to get away from the empty shops, the rationing and the bombed streets. Besides, her uncle was cattle farming in South Africa, and he encouraged her to enjoy all that the colonies had to offer.

She was involved in the design and building of the new women's ward, with its outdoor exercise yard enclosed by railings that resembled flamingos with elongated necks and legs. She recounted how she used to take her patients on early morning walks in the orange groves and along a jacaranda avenue, which stretched to the boundary of the hospital grounds. She said the age range of her patients went from very young to very old, children mixed in with adults, men mixed in with women. She introduced them to games like grandmother's footsteps and encouraged them to play simple ball games. Winifred said she would never forget three Polish women on her ward who weren't able to speak a word of English. She felt desperately sad for them because they had been shuffled from Poland, through the Middle East and all the way down to Ingutsheni. She had no way of finding out what had happened to make them behave in such bizarre ways. There were other patients who also clung around her ankles, begging for help.

Over the years, Winifred said she introduced teaching programmes so the women could learn to sew and to type. She was horrified that the patients were given mince and sadza served on tin plates at every meal; she complained about there being no fresh vegetables or fruit in their diet. She thought this was incredible, considering the hospital had an arable farm where many of the male patients worked.

Rioting began in the townships near the city centre in the latter part of 1961. Winifred described how her car was stoned by a mob as she drove to work. She managed to run the gauntlet and when she got to the hospital grounds, the warders cheered and shouted, "Come on madam, come on madam!" The police wouldn't let her leave during the middle of the day and one of the men accompanied her home at night. She stayed with friends when the rioting was at its worst.

Winifred fell in love with an American financier. As the rioting grew in intensity, she and Bill decided to go and live in San Francisco. Winifred said a consular official attempted to rape her when she was in the process of applying for an American visa. She locked herself in her flat while this man berated her and tried to break down her door.

Towards the end of 1962, Winifred and Bill emigrated to the USA. A few years later, their relationship ended and Winifred went to live in London where she took up a post as head of the Occupational Therapy Department at St. Bartholomew's Hospital.

Her memories of Ingutsheni helped me see the hospital from her perspective. She did her best to help people at a time when trauma was little understood and electric convulsive therapy was widely practised. As a woman, she deferred to men who held senior positions within the medical profession.

Winifred passed away in 2013. I sometimes wear a delicate gold bracelet, shaped like a flower with diamond-edged petals and a moonstone in the middle, that she gave my mother as a parting gift.

The St. Francis Home for Mentally Handicapped Children was built as part of the hospital in 1958. It was staffed by the Ecclesiastic Sisters of Franciscan Missionaries of the Divine Motherhood. This brought an end to children having to be housed in the main body of the hospital. There were lots of different names for the children at St. Francis: retards, mongols, spastics, idiots, mental defectives, bastards, illegitimate, cretins, knuckleheads, morons, dumbos. My mother said they were unwanted by their parents so the nuns were their guardian angels.

Every year a summer fete was held at St. Francis. The fete filled me and Yael with delirious excitement because the people from Toc H employed a man in a red bowler hat to sell pink candyfloss. My mother drove past the women's ward and up the avenue of jacarandas to St. Francis. The road was like a sheet of corrugated iron in the summer months and the car shook its way over the ruts. We giggled at the way it made our voices vibrate as we drove along. Mother Fatima emerged from the red brick building, her habit a blaze of white, her beaming face framed by a stiff head dress. She didn't seem to mind how it squeezed her chin and made her skin crinkle. Little wisps of grey hair fluttered around her face. She spoke in a soft Irish whisper and did a little curtsy when my father, and then my mother shook her hand. Her head dress made it difficult for her to look down at me, but I saw she had dimples that went in and out when she talked. She wore a long necklace with a shiny silver cross at the bottom. It swayed in a rhythmic way when she walked along next to us and her skirt rustled around her ankles as she led us around the Home. Her trainers squeaked in the silence as we walked along the shiny black corridors. There was a sweet smell which leaked out of the rooms and down the echoing passages.

I didn't like looking at the children and babies lying in their cots. None of them spoke so it was very quiet. Their faces were all twisted and some of them dribbled or had white foamy stuff coming out of their lips. Once, a girl about the same age as me, came and held on to my skirt. When I squirmed and pushed her away, Mother Fatima needed one of the Sisters to come and release the girl's fingers from my dress. The girl wouldn't let go and another Sister appeared and dragged her off. The girl's screams echoed down the corridors. She'd ripped a hole in my pink net petticoat, and I began to cry. Mother Fatima leaned down and smiled her dimpled smile as she straightened up my skirt. Then she gave me a handkerchief with blue forget-me-nots embroidered on it to dry my eyes, while she patted me on the head.

My mother bought me a handknitted Humpty Dumpty. She said the people at Toc H were good at knitting. My Humpty-Dumpty wore a stripy jumper, but his arms and legs were too long and spindly for him to stand on his own. He had a black top hat stitched on the side of his head like a chimney. I took Humpty Dumpty with me on the tractor ride to the hospital farm. Yael and I climbed into an iron trailer behind the old farm tractor. We burned the backs of our legs on the seat because the trailer had been standing in the sun. We were consoled by a Sister who gave us each a toffee apple. The tractor bumped us down the jacaranda avenue, around the hospital buildings, then crunched its way down a black cinder track until, at last, the open fields came into view. The cinders came from the boiler room in the hospital laundry where the patients washed and ironed our clothes. A smell of starch blasted out of the open doors. We stopped at a deserted cow shed and were forbidden from running into the fields, where rows of strawberries stretched away into the distance. I remember how the air above the plants wobbled in the heat and iron sprinklers poked into the sky. Water sputtered and drifted through the hot air to where we were playing. The earth exhaled warm animal smells and a smell of ripening fruit wafted towards us. We lifted our faces into the cooling spray as each sprinkler swept past us. We played in the empty barns in amongst the hay bales until someone blew a whistle. Then we rattled our way back to St. Francis.

On the way home we sat in the back of the car and ate sticks of candyfloss in silent ecstasy. We squeezed chunks between our muddy fingers until it turned dark pink. The wiry clumps melted instantly inside our mouths. When we got home, Yael and I sat on the black granolith step, still warm from the hot sun of the afternoon. We stuck our tongues out to see whose was dyed a deeper pink. As the last rays slanted across the garden, it was soothing to sit and wait for night to fall. Night apes spied down on us from the eaves of the house, crickets and frogs set up their night- time choruses and fireflies danced above the old iron bucket next to the garden tap. When the red sun slipped away beneath the trees, night fell like a power cut for there were no streetlights at the hospital. The dirt tracks had no names, there were no shops or playgrounds nearby, and our neighbours were safely locked away under bolt and key behind barred windows.

Four

I was fascinated by flying ants that fluttered about after a thunderstorm, depositing their wings in puddles and across the front lawn until it looked like it was covered in confetti. There were bright green praying mantises in the hibiscus hedge and millipedes we called 'chongololos' which wove their way out of the under-growth into the broiling sunshine. 'Chongies' were easy to catch because as soon as you touched them, they rolled themselves up into a coil. I used to put a rolled up chongie on my hand and sit on the front step, waiting for it to unravel itself. It would uncurl and tickle its way up my arm, its legs feathering themselves along, to make its way around the back of my neck. I used to chase the dog away from a chongie sleeping contentedly in the sun. It upset me if anything dented their shells because their blood was yellow, not red.

A tabby cat came to live in the garage and slept amongst some dusty Hessian sacks. My mother named her 'Mother Pussy' when it was clear that she was about to have kittens. I remember my mother guiding my fingers across the expansive mound of Mother Pussy's stomach so that I could feel them moving underneath her skin. I can still see those delightful kittens with their newly opened blue eyes and their miniature pointy tails as they staggered and played around their dozing mother. I remember their ecstasy as they kneaded and purred and mewled over her in the musty light of the garage. I remember the sweet smells of milk and warmly licked fur as she groomed and fussed over her tiny kittens. My father took to calling me 'Little Miss Pussy' for he noticed my joy at cradling the kittens in my arms and carting them about the garden. And so, one unforgettable day, it was a total horror when I found all the kittens dead in the garage and Mother Pussy gone and lost to me forever. My mother said a wild dog had got into the garage at night. My father said he had caught Mother Pussy eating one of her own dead kittens and so he had chased her away. I had nightmares about headless kittens for months afterwards.

It was my birthday treat to be taken to the circus. I remember the magical moment of going inside the creamy tent with its golden sawdust ring. The interior of the tent was warm and welcoming after the icy winter mornings at that time of year, when frost turned the wild grasses and the lawns a silvery-grey.

I watched the elephants chasing along, holding onto each other's tails with their trunks. I was captivated by the white circus horses and loved the way they bowed their heads and snorted as they cantered around the ring. At the crack of a whip they jumped, trotted, or stood to attention, their front legs waving to me in the audience. They didn't miss a beat when girls in tutus jumped onto their backs and did acrobatics. The sequins on their costumes sparkled, their bright faces beamed, and the horses seemed content to gallop endlessly around in circles. I held my breath as the acrobats swung upside down above us. To the roll of drums, they flew through the air and I sat on the edge of my seat as they saved each other from plummeting down to earth. There were no safety nets in those days.

When I outgrew the circus, my mother took me to watch the show jumping at the Trade Fair in the Show Grounds. I made jumps around the garden and Yael galloped along behind me. We strung pieces of string between garden chairs and made courses around the lawn. We jumped over everything – the stone walls along the flower beds, in and out of the concrete sandpit under the thatched shelter, through the water sprinkler, even up and down the corridors of the house.

My first teacher, Mrs. Mackay, read us Robert Louis Stevenson's poetry. I dreamed of having a horse that I would name Counterpane, who would gallop me through the tall grass, all the way to school and back home again.

Albert Lamorisse's film about a wild stallion named White Mane left a lasting impression on me. Set in The Camargue where horses gallop freely, a boy befriends a white stallion and helps it escape the clutches of a group of men trying to capture it and break it in. The film ends with

White Mane and the boy galloping away into the waves and escaping forever.

At the beginning of 1961 we got a black and white television set and a whole world of stories was suddenly available to me, right there in our living room. My father was forever fiddling with its aerial to stop the picture from turning into wavy lines. I longed to have a horse like the Lone Ranger's. Silver would come when I whistled, and we would race like the wind to do good works. I would have a smiling friend like Tonto galloping beside me.

My fantasies about horses continued until one awful day in 2010 when my daughter had a serious riding accident. Her horse suddenly spooked, sending her flying to the ground. As it galloped off, its rear hoof clipped the side of her head. I took her to hospital, one side of her head swollen out of all proportion and her right eye bloodied and closed. In the event she wasn't seriously injured and recovered well. The accident made me reflect deeply about my passion for horses and the realities of riding them.

Five

My mother owned a series of bulldogs when we lived at Ingutsheni. Hardy was the first and soppiest one. He was named after the English novelist Thomas Hardy. He was a white bulldog with a brindle face and floppy jaws. One morning I went to examine some ant bear holes at the bottom of our drive, and Hardy was lying nearby, dozing in the middle of the road. I saw Mr. Radcliffe's silver jaguar drive around the corner and come down the road towards me. I assumed he would stop when he got closer to me and the dog lying in the road. Mr. Radcliffe drove straight over the sleeping bulldog, turned left, crossed the bridge over an open sewer and was gone. The car made clouds of dust, but I could see Hardy squirming around. He was making an awful howling noise. I ran as fast as my legs would carry me into the house to find my mother. I found her in the kitchen, and she came running, with flour on her hands and her apron flying from her neck. She held the dog's head in her lap. I remember his poor old chin was dotted with blood, and dust, and bits of sand. He was still squirming about and making a whimpering noise. My mother sent me to find Shadrick our 'house boy'. She said he was to bring a sheet from the linen cupboard. They wrapped Hardy up in it and Shadrick carried the crying dog and put him on the backseat of my mother's car. She drove off in a hurry. I thought Hardy was going to die so I went and hid under my eiderdown. But, a few hours later, he came back home from the vets, alive and snuffling as usual.

Mr Radcliffe came to drink whisky with my parents - that's why I recognised his car. He always patted me on the head and smelled of au de cologne and peppermints. He wore a dark blue suit with grey stripes on it. A pink handkerchief peeped out of his top pocket and matched his cravat with its pink and maroon paisley pattern. He was older than my parents and spoke with an English accent like my mother's.

My mother mentioned George Radcliffe in her diary. Her entry on 11th January 1980 says: *"G. Radcliffe died, a brave, kind man – death is a kind relief."*

Mr. Radcliffe didn't live in the grounds of the hospital like we did. Maybe he didn't want to mix with the Afrikaners and Irish people who lived there. It's more likely it was because he was a bachelor. A male nurse was entitled to a house if he had a family to support. The male nurses lived in a dusty compound over the road from the nurses' home. The female nurses and the hospital matron lived in a large building which had a private tennis court to one side of it. The court was made of tarmac; sometimes Yael and I went and kicked a ball around on it. My mother forbad us to go to the male nurses' houses because of the Calhouns. Mrs. Calhoun had invited her over for tea once and she'd been horrified to see a monkey tied to a tree in their backyard. The monkey had screeched at her in a horrendous way. On one occasion she'd seen the Calhoun children throwing rocks at it and tormenting it.

When I was older, one of the Calhoun boys invited me to a school dance. When he came to the door, I ran and hid underneath my bed. I made Yael go and tell him I couldn't come with him because I had sunstroke.

Anton van Zyl, the caretaker at the hospital, lived in a bungalow on the corner of the dirt track which led to our house. The Van Zyl's house was almost entirely covered by a bougainvillea creeper. When we drove past their bungalow, I used to think of the Sleeping Beauty and the prince who had to chop his way through all those brambles to reach her. My mother told us that one of Anton's relatives was such a top-class tennis player that she'd played at Wimbledon.

Opposite the Van Zyl's lived the hospital pharmacist, known as 'Bulldog' Brewer. Elaine and Justine went to the same school as the Brewer children and were sometimes invited over to their house for a swim. The Brewer's swimming pool was a large metal tank with steps up one side. The house was hidden away behind a rubber hedge whose rubbery fingers formed an impenetrable barrier. So dense was the shade in the spot where the swimming tank stood that the water inside it was as black as ink.

To get to my father's office, we drove past the Brewer's house and around a corner. We often saw European men in striped pyjamas, playing bowls on a green next to the administration building. We weren't allowed inside the office block. Yael and I had to wait in the car, where we bickered in the sweltering heat while my mother disappeared inside. My father's office was next to the front door, above which an ornate blue plaque dated 1943 with an angular bird on it caught one's eye. We could see an enormous wooden fan twirling around on the ceiling in his office. We sat and watched it churn its way through the hot air while we waited for what seemed forever until our mother reappeared and drove us home.

Six

Our Granny Alice sent Elaine a book about southern African butterflies. My father got ether from the hospital so Elaine could kill the butterflies she caught by putting them in a glass jar filled with ether. She mounted them on a sheet of cork board, using paper strips to make their wings stretch out and stay flat. When our granny came to visit, she took photos of Elaine's collection. I remember how proud I felt when Elaine once let me take her collection to school for a science exhibition.

Granny Alice brought all of us presents when she came to visit in 1959. Elaine got a combustion engine which shunted along by itself. My father got it going it with a flick of his cigarette lighter. Thin wisps of smoke unfurled from its funnel as it steamed across the room. We got a tinker toy set to share but there was only one wooden hammer. My father put it away for Yael when he was older, and I watched the pair of them build rockets, and diggers, and motor cars out of red, green, blue and yellow sticks. Justine and I were given blow-up dolls called hug-a-bugs. Mine was black and Justine's was white. Granny Alice blew into mine and turned it into a squeaky baby. She said it looked just like the piccanins who were strapped onto their mothers' backs with blankets. My hug-a-bug hung off my arm like a Kaola bear. It had an open mouth and one of its eyes looked like it was winking. It had two hollow loops for ears and a painted curl on its forehead. I took it into the bath with me and washed it with Lifebuoy soap, like Mary did when she washed her baby. I put the hug-a-bug on my lap so it could listen to the story about Little Black Sambo, who was chased by some tigers around a tree. Little Black Sambo ran so fast round the tree that the tigers gradually melted into one another and turned into golden yellow butter. I sang songs to my hug-a-bug about Noddy and the Gollywog, and I would spank its bottom for splashing water out of the bath.

Granny Alice also gave me an Indian doll with jet black hair tied back with a leather thong. I loved its soft leather dress with tassels along the bottom. The doll had a leather papoose on its back but there was no baby in it. The papoose didn't look nearly as warm and comfortable as the blanket Mary wore to carry her baby around, snoozing on her back. Granny Alice gave Yael a collection of Matchbox cars. She took Yael to Haddon and Sly to buy a doll because he wanted one like my Indian doll.

My grandmother made us milk shakes with a hand whisk. She used food colouring to make 'green mambas', 'brown cows' and 'pink elephants'. She and my mother made play dough that we pummelled in the kitchen while it was still warm. Granny Alice was as stout as our nannies and her hair hung in a grey sheet down her back. In the daytime she threaded it into a thin grey plait. She wound the plait around and around her head, so it made an alice-band and a hat at the same time. Elaine and Justine made her plait their hair so in the photographs they all look very pleased with themselves. My hair was too short for plaits, so I got one of my sisters to make a long plait out of grey wool. I hung it over my head and used my sun hat as an anchor. I watched my woolly plaits flying along next to me as I spun myself around in the sunshine.

Part One

Our bungalow had a corrugated iron roof which the men from Public Works Department painted silver. My father spoke Afrikaans to the men who brought Africans in white overalls with them to do the work. Yael and I watched as they painted the outside of the house a chalky white. Our bedroom, with its swirling burglar bars, was painted a creamy yellow. A smell of paint kept us awake at night until the heat of the day baked the house dry. At night the corrugated iron roof cracked and groaned as it cooled down. This frightened us until our mother told us it was only the roof getting used to being out of the blistering sun.

The flamboyant tree dropped red flowers until a thick carpet lay beneath it. It produced pods as big as boomerangs which fell to the ground in the winter. Yael and I threw them like helicopters across the lawn. When we banged them against our hands, the seeds inside them rattled like maracas. When I got strong enough to break a pod over my knee, we lined up the seeds to look at the wings they were beginning to sprout. When the pods burst, the wind blew them like spinning tops around the garden.

I used to pick flowers and mix up medicines in a tin mug. I made potions out of all the flowers I picked - violets, orange poppies, white pansies, deep red verbena, yellow nasturtiums and pale blue forget-me-nots. If I got the combination right. I dreamed I'd be able to fly with the birds and the butterflies, which glided so effortlessly around the garden. The beds along the driveway and around the front lawn spilled their petals like confetti when ferocious gusts of wind heralded the arrival of a late afternoon thunderstorm.

My mother's rose garden with its red, pink and cream blooms smelled like heaven on hot days. The roses grew between a thatched shelter and an old wall where Elaine ran about hitting a tennis ball against it in the endless sunshine. A palm tree towered above the shelter and an ivy-covered bird bath lay in the cool of its shade. The tree spewed great talons of leaves high up above its matted trunk. Plumes of oily nuts nestled in its highest recesses and fell to earth like yellow marbles after torrential showers. Yael and I liked to skid around on their slippery skins as they lay rotting on the crazy paving, and the air beyond the shade wobbled in a wall of heat.

The window in our parents' bedroom looked out over the front garden. Below a pale blue window ledge, a creamy pink frangipani bush attracted so many butterflies, wasps and bees that it resembled a railway station frequented by miniature passengers. On a still summer's day, its pungent scent drifted up into my parents' bedroom where it mingled with the smells of my father's aftershave and my mother's perfumes. The aromas of 'Apple blossom', 'blue grass' and 'old spice' bring back the joy I felt when I lay between them as they read their newspapers, smoked their cigarettes and sipped their tea which had been delivered by one of our servants on a wooden tray. A sweet silence lay between us, when the only sound was the rustling of the newspaper mixed with the tender feel of softening starch on the crumpled sheets on their bed.

Justine played a tune called 'chopsticks' on an old piano on the veranda. I remember my father dancing around with my feet on top of his as Justine laughed and played it faster and faster. Elaine says the house was full of books, music and games when we were all young. I remember how my father used to hold me over a flower bed when I needed to do a wee and how I used to fret about it, especially after my mother said a wasp might mistake my bottom for a lovely white flower.

Seven

When I was five, we went on holiday to Cape Town where we met up with my grandmother. It gave Lionel a chance to show her and my mother his native city before my grandmother sailed on to India. The excitement of the train journey to Cape Town is still palpable. It was such a treat for me and Yael to sleep in the same compartment as our parents, while Elaine and Justine shared a smaller cabin next door.

We were taken to the station in 'The Safari', the hospital bus. I remember the busy shopping district next to the station, with masses of people milling about, the women wearing brightly coloured head scarves (doeks) and the men standing in groups, chatting and smoking cigarettes. Women carried baskets, fruit, and laundry on their heads with babies dozing on their backs, their heads wobbling from side to side as they walked along talking and gesticulating with their friends.

The sight of the train waiting, smoke hissing out of the engine, sent Yael and I into a delirium of anticipation. Elaine and Justine disappeared inside our carriage and we had to be helped up the iron steps. Inside our compartment, Yael and I patted the green leather seats and stroked the polished wooden panels. The train pulled slowly out of the station making huge bursts of smoke. We stood in the corridor and waved goodbye to the cars and people. The scene outside our window slowly gave way to grassland and thorn trees. With the train firmly on its way, Yael and I arranged leather bolsters from the seats along the corridor next to our cabin. We hurtled up and down, oblivious to the motion of the carriage as it clattered its way to the Rhodesian border.

When the train pulled wearily to a stop at Mafeking in Bechuanaland (now the Republic of Botswana) a gaggle of people ran alongside. Ragged people with woolly hair and bare feet. Women with old cloths wrapped around their heads and babies tied on their backs with towels and blankets. They called up to us as we stood peering down at them. Hands held up carvings of wild animals and spears and three-legged stools. Women held up crocheted tablecloths and place mats. Boys pushed along toys made of wire and wood, with wheels made out of bottle tops and other bits and pieces. Girls waved necklaces and bangles made out of red lucky beans and tiny glass beads. Eyes pleaded, mouths moved and clouds of flying insects hovered around them. Flies flitted onto trails of snot around noses and made sorties into upturned eyes; they buzzed around heads and settled on lips and hands and feet. My mother bought a creamy tablecloth for her friend Betty and a wooden lion for me. Its mane was made from monkey fur and its tail was blackened by fire. Years later it still smelled of wood smoke and something dead. Justine chose a tortoise carved out of dark wood. Its tiny head had two white dots for eyes and its shell was beautifully patterned. Elaine got a lucky bean necklace and Yael a carved wooden spear. A whistle blew and the crowd below pressed in closer and waved things more frantically. Final cries and pleading went up over the sea of people as the train started its slow departure from Mafeking. We hung out of the window, watching them give chase until, finally, the train picked up speed and they were left far behind.

My father wasn't interested in the marketplace outside the train and we ran off to show him our treasures. We found him in the dining car where he sat smoking and reading a newspaper. I remember Justine let me hold her wooden tortoise in exchange for my lion and I traced the patterns on its back with my tongue. My father snatched it away and yelled "agh siss man Charlotte!" He said if I wasn't careful, I'd catch some 'bladdy awful kaffir disease'.

My mother opened the window in our compartment just a sliver so that the smuts – tiny bits of coal from the furnace inside the engine – which flew out of its chimney as it snorted and clattered its way across the Karoo desert, wouldn't catch in our eyelashes or spatter our crisp white sheets with a layer of soot. The train huffed and puffed its way across the monotonous landscape, its wheels drumming and echoing in a melodic and mesmerising way.

At mealtimes we followed our parents into the dining car, where the tables were set with silver cutlery and polished gravy dishes. My parents shook out thickly starched napkins and stuffed them down our fronts. Waiters swayed rhythmically with the motion of the train and served us our food, their white uniforms as starched as the tableware. They used forks and spoons like tongs to deliver meat and vegetables onto our plates.

The train whistled through the days and nights of our journey. We slept in bunk beds freshly made each morning by African attendants. My father and Yael slept on the two bottom bunks. Being on the bunk above enabled me to lie on my stomach and peer into the darkness through the shutters, which made the cabin as dark as a cupboard. I remember waking up every time the train slowed to halt. Then I waited in eager anticipation for the train to start moving again. It moved so slowly at first the only way to tell it was moving was to look at something like a rooftop or a tree, to see whether it was us moving or a train gliding off alongside us. It caused a strange sensation inside my head, as if my body was being left behind. The same thing happened when the train came into a station. It seemed to take forever for it to slow down to a complete stop.

My mother said it gave her the kittens if I put my head too far out of the window to try to see the platform. She gripped my skirt in case I fell out. I remember waking up on the last morning of our journey to look out of the window at vineyards and mountains in amazement. It felt as if we'd got there by magic and we'd arrived in a new and enchanted land.

We stayed with the Boschoff's for a few days. Mr. Boschoff worked for the World Health Organisation. He regularly visited Rhodesia to sit on the General Medical Council, along with my father and other members of the medical profession. Mr. Boschoff sat me on his knee and nuzzled me with his beaky nose; I didn't like his yellow teeth or the smelly pipe he clamped between them when he talked. He sang 'eeny weeny itsy bitsy polka dot bikini' to Elaine and Justine when they took us to swim at Muizenberg. They drove us to the Steenbrass Dam singing 'She'll be coming round the mountain when she comes'. I wanted to be sick because they'd taken us up Table Mountain the day before and the cable car being so high off the ground had terrified me. There was something about the inky black water in the Steenbrass Dam below me that filled me with terror. Looking back, I see I associated that colour with the ink in my first fountain pen as I struggled to form my letters. I drew ships with angular bodies and funnels spewing plumes of smoke, just like the ones I'd seen from the top of Table Mountain, drifting far below me. I drew horses' heads, seen side-ways, with feminine fringes and curly eye lashes.

My parents borrowed the Boschoff's car and drove us to Gordon's Bay where we stayed at the van Riebeck Hotel. The warm Indian Ocean lapped against the sands of a flat beach over the road from the hotel. Elaine remembers my father played ping-pong endlessly with her and Justine, while Yael and I went to the toy shop with my mother to buy buckets and spades and sweets. I remember my father's delight in eating watermelon konfyt and koeksisters dripping with golden syrup. He smacked his lips and said they reminded him of home.

I floated on my lilo in the shallow water, watching crabs scuttling around in the crystal-clear water underneath me. Neither of my parents could swim and so I guess the shallows had a soothing effect on them. The first few days drifted along in a peaceful way, until one morning when Elaine floated a long way off on her lilo. My father shouted and ran in a frenzy over the water to get her. After that I became afraid of the crabs because they churned up the sand behind them in the same way my father's feet had done as he raced through the water to get Elaine. I refused to get on my lilo in case it sailed me out to sea.

During the train journey home, I had a fight with my father over breakfast. I didn't like the eggs and fried tomato he ordered because the toast had gone soggy and it made me gag. Nothing would persuade me to eat it. In our compartment that night I heard my father say I was 'a bladdy little pest'. He said he hadn't wanted to have 'any more bladdy kids', it was my mother's idea not his.

The next morning, I watched him as he snipped his moustache in the mirror. He winked at me sitting behind him, but all I could see were the pointy tips of his scissors. The train had lost its music as it thundered along.

Eight

Yael and I could hear people moaning and crying through the hibiscus hedge that separated our house from the hospital buildings. Sometimes, we crept into the hedge to see who was wailing so pitifully. We could see the exercise yard with its wrought iron flamingos. It seemed as if the birds were responsible for the racket going on behind them. Occasionally we caught sight of a bedraggled grey head or a pair of feet shuffling along in fluffy slippers. Other times a person would hang onto the bars and make such ear-splitting screams that we ran off to hide in the house. They sounded like the grey lowrie birds whose harsh voices called "gwaa gwaa - go away, go away" or the black crows that squawked at each other from the top of the rubber hedge, often dive-bombing my father's white Mini, when he drove around the corner to his office.

The bedroom I shared with Yael was next to a rubber hedge which separated our bungalow from the superintendent's mansion next door. The hedge squeaked and creaked in an alarming way when a storm was brewing. Sometimes the wind blew so strongly that it ripped whole branches off and spewed them on the ground. We picked them up and dipped our fingers in the sticky white sap that oozed out to see how it made our fingers stick together. The sight of it made my mother shout. She frog-marched us into the kitchen and made us wash our hands in the sink because she said the rubber hedge sap was poisonous. She said we'd go blind if we got it in our eyes.

Elaine and Justine teased us that the creaking rubber hedge was really a wicked old witch whose knees squeaked. They said the witch shut herself up in the wendy-house outside our bedroom window and hid underneath the floorboards when daybreak came. Yael used to grind his teeth in his sleep and the sound of that, along with the creaking hedge, made me lie awake at night. I dreamed that Yael ground his teeth so that they grew as sharp as the witch's teeth. When sounds in the night frightened me, I used to wind my sheet around my head. There I'd lie, as still as a statue, thinking of the witch whose squeaky knees kept time with the creaking rubber hedge as it did battle with the wind.

One night I was woken up by sharp flashes of lightning. It was pitch black in our bedroom. I lay and watched the room light up as if someone was flicking a switch on and off. So bright was each flash I could clearly see the enormous wooden fan above me. Then I heard another sound which made my heart race. It was the sound of Yael cracking and grinding his teeth. Another flash of lightning was followed by a forceful gust of wind, which made the rubber hedge outside the window creak in a meaningful way. An ear tingling crackle meant a stupendous crash of thunder was about to split the heavens. I scrambled out of bed and raced down the dark passage to my parents' bedroom. A clap of thunder like a volcanic explosion made the hairs on the back of my neck stand on end. Yael started to wail and so did I.

My father was already out of bed. He snatched me up and stumbled with me under one arm. I squirmed around and tried to run back to my mother. He threw me onto my bed and another flash of lightning lit up his face. I saw his grey hair all tousled and wild; he didn't look like my father at all. I screamed and he smacked me so hard I bounced off the bed and hit my head on the wall. He carried on hitting me and told me to stop making such a bladdy noise or I would wake up the whole bladdy hospital. Then he stumbled off to bed.

Lightning continued to strobe the room. Thunder ripped through the air with such violence that the bars on the windows jangled. Then it rumbled like an angry voice grumbling off into the distance. In another flash of lightning, I looked over at Yael's bed and saw he was gone. In that moment, I knew my mother had followed along behind my father and taken Yael back to bed with her. I lay still and held my breath. The rain battered the iron roof and drowned out every other sound.

After what seemed an eternity, some frogs started to sing. Soon, their raucous voices filled the darkness with a strangely calming noise. After that, when thunder and lightning bombarded our bedroom and the rain drummed like a fiend on the iron roof, I held my breath and waited. As soon as the frogs' chorus began, I knew the world was a safe place again. As their croaky voices grew in number, sleep would eventually come and claim me.

Blue Remembered Sky

PART TWO

Inmates

The effect of lobotomy, at best, was to induce passivity and diminish individuality.

At worst, it turned a mentally distressed person into a brain-damaged one.

Some patients, excruciatingly aware that something was lost, described it as being de-souled.

But the staff at the hospital continue to insist, as they attend the zombified survivors, that the operation is worthwhile – indeed, they hold it out as a hope of salvation.

Hilary Mantel –
Foreword to Faces in the Water by Janet Frame

But here you had to provide your own bandages from within yourself to bind wounds that could not be seen or measured, and at the same time it seemed you had to forget that the patients were people, for there were so many of them and there was so much to do.

The remedy was to shout and hit and herd.

Janet Frame

"Can I come down there [to Ingutsheni] and try some of my medicines?"
Jack Makwayo in a letter to the Superintendent

Lynette A. Jackson

Blue Remembered Sky

Part Two

One

Towards the end of 1960 my family moved into the superintendent's house next door. The new superintendent didn't want to live at the hospital, so my father was given the house. It had Dutch gables and a colonnaded veranda overlooking two sweeping lawns. Bulawayo city centre lay in the distance over a vast area of flaxen grasses and thorn trees. A round fishpond with a domed roof created a roundabout at the end of the long sandy driveway to the house. One evening, as Yael and I pushed our cars along the driveway, we drew near to our old home. We heard a boy singing 'Figaro'. Here was a sound we could copy without Elaine yelling at us to stop. We scampered back up to the house. Yael cupped his chubby hands around his mouth, and we stood on the top lawn. "Figaro, Figaro, Figaro" we sang. Our voices sailed over the silver corrugated roof of the house, above its Dutch gables edged in soft blue, out towards Bulawayo and up into the Heavens. The wailing people over the road were gone.

My mother wrote: *"The Wrights were first in the little house after the superintendent retired and we moved into the Big House. They built the pool. Their children (two girls) were teenagers and we were not all that socially involved. Elaine and Justine went to Townsend with them – Mrs. Wright taught science there. Elaine used to call Dr. Wright 'Little Napoleon'!! She found him very dictatorial – I think!"*

All my memories of my father at the big house are lit by the sunshine which gave him his recreation, lying on his on his reclining plastic sunbed that creaked and squeaked as he lay on it, smoking his cigarettes and twiddling the knobs on his portable radio to get the latest cricket scores. I remember how the signature tune for the BBC Overseas Service wafted through the hot air, and white butterflies drifted over the flowerbeds like tails on an invisible kite. Grey hairs on his bare chest glittered with sweat and the wrinkles guttering his stomach leaked when he sat up to fit a cigarette into its holder. He huffed and puffed in the heat, breathing smoke out of his nose. He's always on the top lawn in my memories, his eyes hidden by his tear drop dark glasses and his nose as red as a beacon. When the sky was grey, the house was filled with gloom when he sat in the lounge wearing his herringbone slacks and wool jumper and we did our best to keep out of his way. How I longed for the sun to shine, when he came in for lunch, bright red, smiling, smudges of Sea and Ski sun cream filling the wrinkles on his forehead.

I look at a photograph of my parents together on the top lawn. My mother, in her sleeveless cotton dress is standing next to my father on his recliner. Even on those sweltering afternoons, she wore cloudy stockings that made her legs silky and smooth. The air around them was secretive. Snatches of conversation would drift over to me sitting high up in a tree on the other side of the lawn while they smoked and chatted. "Ja …. Hell …" I heard my father laugh in between my mother's mumblings. After a while, I would creep down from my branch to land neatly in the cool shadow beneath the tree. I'd pick up my discarded butterfly net and be off on a chase in pursuit of my quarry, oblivious of the hot sand under my bare feet as I tracked my way through the singing grasses.

There were no servants around to serve us on the weekends. The house was silent, especially in the kitchen. On weekdays the servants sat chatting on an old sheet, shelling peas and polishing the silver before they went inside to cook and lay out the table things.

Those memories twirl around me, and somewhere in between is the time my father had all his teeth out and came home with a plastic smile.

Two

A large stone relief in the form of an angular bird was prominent above the front door of the superintendent's house and on the front of the administration block where my father had his office. The bird's image, the national emblem, was on our coins, paper money and the national flag. It adorned the covers of guidebooks, history books and lots of other things. The Zimbabwe bird was, and still is, a powerful spiritual icon.

My father's study served as the television room; it was a cosy refuge after supper. There I spent most evenings watching whatever was on TV. I watched Mohammed Ali, Sugar Ray Leonard and all-in wrestlers, with peroxided hair and body-hugging swimming costumes, throwing each other out of an elasticated boxing ring.

How well I remember the Cartwright brothers riding gallantly out of the blazing map of their Ponderosa ranch at the beginning of Bonanza. I sat captivated by the wagons which rolled along through thunderstorms in Rawhide, and I fell in love with the Lone Ranger and Tonto.

How I laughed at the stupid American soldiers in F Troop who were always having dealings with even stupider Red Indians called the 'Hekarwees'. The Hekarwees were so named for saying "where the heck are we?" because they were so stupid. The 'Red Skins' in the westerns that I loved watching were gunned down with gay abandon, while the cow-boys lasso-ed horses, cows and women without so much as a cut or a bruise on their manly bodies.

I watched American comedies like The Flying Nun, Hogan's Heroes, the Beverley Hill Billies, the Addams Family, and sitcoms like Bewitched, the Mary Tyler Moore Show, Phyllis Diller, Red Skelton, Bob Hope, The Benny Hill Show and I Love Lucy. Then there were English shows like Muffin the Mule, Sooty and Sweep, and Dr Who. I adored Mr. Spock and James T. Kirk in Star Trek as they sailed around the universe in the starship Enterprise 'to boldly go where no man had been before'.

Every year, I sat up all night watching the Mayor's Christmas Cheer Show and I never missed Top of the Pops. The unfolding story of The Fugitive, starring David Janssen as Dr Richard Kimble, a man on the run after being accused of murdering his wife, was essential viewing. Every week justice eluded Dr. Kimble who, with the help of Lieutenant Phillip Gerard, hunted for a one-armed man witnessed fleeing the scene of the murder. I watched Alfred Hitchcock's psychological thriller Psycho late one night. As I crept back to my bedroom, I stopped to use the toilet and there, on the floor of the shower cubicle, my cat had left some muddy pawprints. For a split second, the terror of the shower scene came to mind and the creepy music screeched in my ears. I raced back to my bedroom with my heart pounding.

I remember listening with amusement to Wrex Tarr and his comedy sketches. Tarr became a popular comedian, having started out as a news reader for the Rhodesian Broadcasting Corporation. He made two successful LP records called 'Futi Chilapalapa' and 'The Cream of Chilapalapa' in which he made fun of how Africans spoke English. He used a language which was known as 'kitchen kaffir' or 'chilapalapa'. This language was also known as 'fanakalo'. It was derived mostly from IsiZulu and it included bits of English, Afrikaans and ChiShona words. The prefix 'chi' signfies the speaker of a particular African dialect, and the word 'lapa' means 'there' in chiShona.

I loved watching the Mod Squad. When Clarence Williams III was on the screen, my father would laugh and say "There's that enigmatic kaffir! Good old enigmatic!" Our servants had English names, or were given names like 'Innocent', 'Tuppence' or 'Poison'. The Africans I knew at the hospital had no surnames.

The word 'kaffir' was an Arabic word to describe an 'unbeliever' or 'non-muslim', and it was used by Arab slavers who bought and sold the indigenous black people of Africa during the slave trade.

It has been sad to learn that a skin whitening cream sold by Amba Products was used by African women during the 1950's and 1960's; this cream caused irreversible skin damage. Patricia Battye, a social worker, fought a lengthy and successful campaign to have Amba Products banned.

Such was the power of propaganda, that I had no idea who Robert Mugabe or Nelson Mandela were, nor did I know the names of any black activists, actors or academics when I was growing up in Rhodesia. My parents regarded Africans as lesser beings whose place in the world was to serve and submit to white people and our so-called 'superior' approach to life. I remember when I visited Elaine in the UK for the first time in 1978, I was astounded to hear Africans who could speak 'the Queen's English'. I was amazed at the dullness of the skies, the punk rockers with their pink and green hair and the grey buildings. I was equally astounded to see a black person holding hands with a white person. My father had said he would disown me if I had sexual intercourse with a black man. He said a mixed-race child would be no child of his. He said "You'll need your head read for bringing a bastard like that into the world".

Three

Newton and Martin were the 'guard boys' who brought a squad of men over from the hospital. Yael wrote: *"I do remember the guards and patients. The guards were Martin and Newton. Marupa used to clean the patio and steps - best floor polisher I've ever seen! He had white hair – he was a sweet man who used to sing whilst he worked. The only other one I remember well was Gonrogh – we used to call him Gone Wrong. He used to work tirelessly and shouted loudly every now and then. Martin always used to tell me his bicycle was a motor bike and that Susan was his transistor radio! He wasn't as friendly as Newton and he was also sterner with the patients".*

Justine wrote: *"As soon as you said "Marupa" I had an image of his thin bony face, soft silvery hair and that tight dry black skin. It's funny how one's memory comes back straight away at the name. You're right, he was a quiet dignified man - shame what a life. Of course, lots of what you said brought back so many memories that I hadn't given a single thought to for hundreds of years, it really feels like that was someone else's life completely, it's so far removed from today. It also brought back the sadness I used to feel when those poor things lined up for their cigarettes. What a strange life that was for children to have. Anyway, I think we've all survived amazingly well."*

The inmates tramped a path through the mealie field with their bare feet. They trooped along with one guard at the front and the other at the back. They worked all morning until a gong signalled it was time for them to file back to the hospital for lunch. They returned for an afternoon shift until five o'clock, when the guards marched them back again.

Yael and I used to loiter around the servants' quarters behind the garage, where the guards and our servants rolled their cigarettes and sipped their tea out of tin mugs.

Part Two

The inmates sat in a silent group under a tree next to an old tennis court until Martin or Newton sounded the gong and sent them back to their chores. The guards talked and laughed as they squatted with our servants around the fire. They shared out old bits of newspaper and tobacco to make into cigarettes. Newton's grey moustache was yellowed at either end from trailing his tongue up and down to lick his cigarettes shut as the paper burned its way down. On cold winter days Yael and I stood close to the fire and dipped our marie biscuits into their tea. They lit their cigarettes in the hot coals and stood about in the winter sunshine, puffing on them and telling stories with words which clicked and spluttered with laughter.

The inmates swept leaves off the driveway and grass clippings off the lawns with their straw brooms. Justine said they looked like witches. My father said that witch doctors were a 'bladdy nuisance with all their hokus pokus'. He said they were making people 'more penga than they were already' with their talk of curses and evil spirits. He laughed about them throwing bones and said they were a bunch of superstitious bastards. He said the af's had a long way to go before they got anywhere near being as civilised as us. My father said what with bladdy witchdoctors, terrorists and bladdy prostitutes, he was having a hard time coping with the number of mad kaffirs who were being admitted for treatment. I remembered our granny had told us stories about witches who liked to cook children and eat them. Yael and I looked at the size of the inmates and decided they were too big to fly around on their brooms.

We used to horse around with them and made them give us piggy backs around the garden. The inmates wore pale blue shorts and shirts, with a dark brown jumper in the winter. Their shaved heads twinkled with beads of sweat as they went about their chores. As the sun rose in the sky, sweat ran in streams down their cheeks while the guards stood watching them underneath their wide brimmed hats. In the winter the inmates' legs were covered in goose-bumps because their old brown jumpers were full of holes and they didn't wear knee high khaki socks like the guards did. They were always bare-foot, come rain, or frost, or shine. They moved languidly around the garden, giving an occasional shout or doing a sudden dance.

On hot days, the inmates lined up at the garden tap while each man dunked his watering-can into a rusty metal drum. The muscles in their arms bulged and the water left bleeding trails in the red dust as they slopped off to water my mother's flowers. Sometimes they fitted sprinklers to the ends of their cans and watered the old tennis court with weed killer. Two men pulled a heavy metal roller behind the one who was doing the watering. The sweat poured off them and made dark rivers run down their necks and down their legs. The yellow sand on the court was the same colour as the wide cracks in their heels. Yael laughed and said it was the way God made muntu's feet. The tops of their feet turned pale grey with dust as they swept.

My memories of living at the big house revolve around Newton, Martin, Marupa, Ntete, Gonrogh, and Mapicke. Mapicke was young and strong and he was exceptionally silent. So obliging was he that the guards used him for all the strenuous chores. It was Mapicke who dug the square holes with an iron pickaxe when my mother wanted to plant a new rose bush. It was Mapicke who mowed the lawns, rolled the court and humped heavy wheelbarrows around the garden. Like all the inmates, the whites of his eyes looked as if they'd been dyed orange. Ntete's eyes were a deep orange, with his bottom lids as dark red as the pomegranate pips Yael and I spat at each other in the orchard beyond the plumbago hedge. There was a sweet medicinal smell about them, mixed in with a strong whiff of body odour. When they gave us piggy backs around the garden we breathed in strong smells of nicotine and sweat.

During a mud ball fight with Yael one afternoon, I accidentally hit Ntete in the face. I stood and watched him shaking his shaved head like a dog does when a fly irritates it. He stood stock still, making clicking noises, and then a stream of unintelligible words came out of his mouth. At first, I did not see I had drawn blood because his skin was so dark. I realised he was bleeding when he turned his head and the sun glinted in the blood running down the side of his face. When I got up close to him, I saw a nasty red dent in his forehead. Ntete did not cry or hold his head; he just picked up his broom and went on sweeping, making clicking sounds with his tongue. He was a short barrel of a person and the skin on his face was so lumpy he seemed to have a permanent case of the goose-bumps. I felt a bit sheepish at what I had done but nobody seemed to mind. The guard boys, if they witnessed it, turned a blind eye and Yael had disappeared. The thrill of the chase was over, and I knew no one would bother to tell my parents.

Every Friday the inmates arrived with clean bundles of laundry balanced on top of their heads. The guards blew their whistles and the caravan of men stopped at the back of the house. The guards told them to put their bundles down outside the kitchen door. The bundles lay where they dropped them, waiting for our servants to unpack them. Our servants stripped our beds and used our dirty sheets to make fresh bundles full of clothes, sheets and anything else that needed to be washed. They put freshly ironed sheets on our beds and sweet-smelling linen around the house. They hung starched towels in the bathroom and put my father's pressed shirts as well as our ironed clothes in the cupboards. At the end of the day the bundles were hefted up and the inmates marched solemnly back to the hospital with our dirty laundry on their heads. I will always wonder who these men were before they were sent to the hospital. Whatever treatment they'd been subjected to made them submissive and zombified. There was no need for the guards to treat them savagely for that had already been done. I console myself that our garden gave them some relief from the wards to which they returned at nightfall, to be locked away until another day dawned and they trooped over to our house.

Yael used to find chameleons in the plumbago hedge. The Africans were terrified of them and rushed off, shouting loudly, to find a stick with which to club them to death. I found a folktale which may explain why they behaved in this way. The story goes that God gave a message about eternal life to a chameleon and instructed it to give the message to First Man. At the same time, God gave a message about mortality to a lizard. As chameleons are so slow and hesitant in the way they move, the lizard delivered its message to mankind first. By the time the chameleon delivered its message to First Man, the spring of eternal life had dried up. Even though First Man went on hands and knees and tried to suck its last remaining drops from the earth, there was nothing left. So, to this day in Africa, chameleons are killed because of man's fury. In order to protect the unfortunate creatures, God endowed chameleons with a magical skin that changes colour and allows them to meld with the background. There was many a time one of the guards would get an inmate to use the sharp end of a spade to chop off a chameleon's head. When I was a child and I caught sight of a chameleon, the blood rushed up into my ears and I ran off in the opposite direction.

Our servants were scared of many things besides chameleons; this included snakes, spiders, wasps and scorpions. They were also terrified of evil spirits. The Ndebele believe in an evil spirit - the untikolotshe (onttikolotshe in the plural). It is thought to be a hairy creature with gouged out eyes and said to be no bigger than a small monkey. Our servants said the untikolotshe liked to bite off peoples' toes while they slept. Their beds were consequently raised off the floor on bricks.

The untikolotshe is so malevolent a spirit that it causes widespread harm wherever it goes. The devil in Christian mythology and the untikolotshe probably have a lot in common.

Four

I made contact with Donald Brewer on Facebook. His father was the hospital pharmacist. Donald was happy to share his memories with me and sent me a detailed map of the hospital grounds.

He wrote: *"White male ward was located behind and was part of the main head office where our fathers worked. The ward and small recreation area were indeed security fenced. The Native and Asiatics/coloured wards were bunched together separated by a gravel road.*

I saw on many occasions native females carrying laundry bundles. There was one female patient who seemed to have no restrictions, as she was considered low risk and heavily medicated on Stemetil, rather pleasant to talk to, coherent and polite. Her name was Daisy. There were two white patients of similar classification to Daisy. Tony Bryce always wore a khaki hat and was also very pleasant to talk to. Then there was Charlie, a Downs Syndrome about twenty years old who used to entertain us with a 'guitar' made out of an old Olivine tin, complete with an attached plank and fishing lines. He used to 'play' and sing - a very happy soul as most of them were. We'd give him fruit and jam sandwiches which he loved. We all had a real soft spot for him.

Yes, I did watch quite a few soccer games and on a number of occasions they'd let me play during practice the day before! As you can see from the sketch there was what appeared to be an old fort which was not visible, surrounded by dense scrub. It was a circular structure contained by bricks perfectly laid. They were not normal house bricks but very like the ones at Khami and Zimbabwe ruins. My Dad didn't seem interested when I told him, so I wonder if it is still there?

The Bulawayo crematorium was a street or two away from Baines School, though I can't remember the street names. I don't remember if it was for whites only or there was another one at Mpilo." (Mpilo Hospital, as opposed to the Bulawayo General Hospital, was for non-white patients only. The word 'Mpilo' means 'life')."

I'd asked Donald if he knew what happened to the inmates when they died. I remember pedalling my bike past the glass doors of the mortuary as I went on my way up the jacaranda avenue to play in an old quarry near the St. Francis Home. It was attached to the high security block. I knew it was a mortuary because there was a hearse parked there most days.

I remember seeing a short, spindly white woman who took a constitutional walk every afternoon to the hospital entrance. Yael called her 'little Miss Nit Wit' and my father said she was 'just another of those bladdy alkies'.

We heard people cheering on Sundays at the soccer pitch. When Yael asked if he could go and watch my father said, "Why would anyone want to go and watch a bunch of crazy kaffirs playing football?" Lionel was equally dismissive of white boys whose parents had helped them escape doing military service. He said they were "a bunch of pooftas". When he had young men referred to him for treatment, he said they got nowhere by pretending they were mentally unfit to fight for the country. He liked to tell us the story of how one of them picked up a soapstone carving of an African man that my mother gave him to use as a paperweight. He threatened to hit my father on the head with it.

My mother concentrated her domestic efforts on spraying her vast collection of rose bushes with sulphur powder to kill green fly. There were over two hundred bushes in our garden, planted in rectangular beds around the fishpond next to Justine's bedroom and on either side of the steps which went down to the lower lawn. Names like Largo, Peace, Super Star and Angel Bells bring back memories of the roses she exhibited at the Horticultural Show. She often won a silver trophy for The Best Bowl in the Show.

I remember how I would wander about the garden with her as the sun sank and the heat of the afternoon began to lift. I remember the tranquillity of a carnelian sky at the end of long hot day. She would snip off a bud and invite me to smell it before laying it in her flower basket. I remember the sound of her secateurs crunching and invisible crickets chirping. I lolled on the grass while the quiet evening air filled with the sounds of her graceful snipping and clipping - interspersed with her inhalations and exclamations.

In the autumn she pruned all the bushes and painted over each stem with her pearly nail varnish to keep out the borer beetles which tunnelled inside to lay their eggs. I remember the pain in her voice if she found that a beetle had found its way through the varnish. She hacked the dead branches off, cursing under her breath and leaving the black branches on the ground for the inmates to pick up. They came and scooped up the thorny debris and wheeled them to the rubbish heap near the tennis court to be burned.

One Easter Sunday, my mother was furious when she discovered the inmates had found the Easter eggs she'd hidden in the garden for us and ate them. Yael and I realised if our mother were the Easter Bunny, she was very likely Father Christmas as well. A week or so before Christmas, we climbed up the back of the garage wall and peered through the rafters into the storeroom behind. There we saw our Christmas presents, waiting to be wrapped.

Five

A burglar broke into our house one night and frightened me for weeks afterwards.

Yael wrote: *"Can't recall much about that night. All I remember was being woken by the sound of the window being pushed open. It had been left ajar. I remember seeing the burglar's head and watching him pull himself up onto the windowsill. He was very agile. He stood on the sill for a very short time and then jumped into our room. He walked past our beds and into the next room. I then heard Lionel shouting and several bangs as the burglar slammed the door into the sitting room. Lionel tried to open it while the burglar held it shut from the other side. That's about it."* Justine remembers how the police came the next morning and dusted everywhere for fingerprints. She wrote: *"I do remember the robbery/break in at the big house. I think the fellow also stole Lionel's tin with the dog on top of it but don't know where that was. I didn't think it was a patient because they didn't go outside until a certain time and this happened either in the night or very early morning - around three or four in the morning. I wish I had a clearer memory but know it was a very scary experience."*

I remember the burglar stealing my father's money box. I've always had the impression the burglar locked my father in his study while he made his getaway. For weeks after the burglary, as I wandered along my favourite paths around the hospital grounds, or pedalled my bike down the dirt tracks, I kept an eye out for my father's money box. I knew he kept a silver revolver in the same drawer as his money. I wondered why the burglar hadn't picked up the revolver, because I remember it was still there when I looked in the drawer. To be on the safe side, I collected up my loose change and put it in one of my mother's old biscuit tins. Then I dug a hole in the field near the kitchen garden and buried it. I guess it's still there.

Justine added: *"What I remember more clearly was Moses being in a fight and Lionel going out with his little gun, then taking poor Moses off to the police station but I don't think it was his fault. It was a fight caused by some other person who had either wandered in or had come back from drinking with Moses, but again it was a scary experience."* Moses worked for my parents as a house boy. He moved with us into suburbia when my father retired in 1971.

One day I stole a box of matches because I wanted to show Yael how to make a fire. We went off behind the car port to collect dry sticks. In my excitement I held a burning match to a low branch on a nearby fir tree. Yael and I watched in horror as flames quickly took hold of the dry pine needles and the whole branch was soon burning out of control. The pine tree turned into an almighty fire ball before we could blink. The blare of cicadas rang in our ears as we raced off to the hospital farm to hide. We waited until our stomachs told us it was time to head home for supper. As we sat around the table, my mother told us how she'd called the fire brigade because the grassland had gone up in flames and the fire had spread rapidly all the way to the hospital entrance. My father said he was sure one of the servants had started it by throwing away a cigarette. He said they were stupid and careless, always setting fire to things. He said 'black bastards couldn't read'; there were plenty of signs around town warning people about throwing cigarettes away without putting them out. Yael and I looked at each other in relief.

The next morning the house was surrounded by a charcoal wasteland which still emitted wisps of white smoke. The blaze was so fierce it had burned down the plumbago hedge along the bottom lawn. The ground crunched underneath our feet when we went to survey the damage.

Six

In 1963, a new family came to live in the bungalow next door. To everyone's delight, their daughter Penny was the same age as me and it wasn't long before we became friends. Her parents, Paddy and Hazel, welcomed me and Yael into their family with open arms. Penny's older brothers, Sean and Dillon, were distant but friendly. Hazel was a church-going Catholic. Penny and her brothers wore their best clothes to Sunday school. They looked as smart as we did when my mother booked for us to eat at The Peking Chinese Restaurant for our birthdays. I remember Penny's confirmation and the tiara she wore in her curly red hair. I remember how her freckles stood out against her crisp white dress and how her black shoes were polished until they shone.

Penny said illegitimate children weren't blessed. She said they went to limbo first and then to purgatory, where they roasted in Hell. She said the children at St. Francis were probably all illegitimate. They were lucky that the Nuns had rescued them, otherwise they'd just be floating around in limbo or being roasted by the devil. She said sinners were people who did bad things, and unless they said they were very sorry to God every time they committed a sin, they were in such serious trouble when they died that they hung around in limbo forever. She said they hadn't reached a state of grace by doing penalties to say they were sorry; some of the very bad ones joined all the illegitimate children in Hell. She had a silver cross on the wall above her bed and a picture of Jesus with his chest torn open and a crown of thorns on his head which made blood pour down his face. All the blood streaming out of Jesus made me look away because I knew he couldn't stay alive for much longer.

Paddy Baxter was a sandy haired man with pale green eyes and a spattering of orange freckles all over his face. Hazel's beehive hairstyle made her seem taller than my mother. She often wore fuchsia coloured lipstick. She had a chocolate-coloured mole above her mouth and her green eyes smiled when she talked. Her nails matched her lipstick and she wore a perfume which smelt of apples. I often heard her calling her cats in the evenings when it was getting dark. She said there were snakes in the tall grasses, and she couldn't rest until they were safe inside the house.

Hazel taught us to make stained-glass pictures out of old sheets of glass. Penny, Yael and I spent hours choosing from the coloured sweet wrappers she carefully smoothed for us to use as backings for the pictures she drew on top of the glass. She made pewter frames decorated with flowers and birds, which she fixed around mirrors. The bungalow next door became a favourite port of call after school and on the weekends. Hazel's cats dozed in the sun and we children chattered around the kitchen table while we made our works of art and Hazel hammered away on her pewter frames.

The Baxters inherited an enormous metal swimming tank from the Wrights. The water inside it was a deep and foreboding shade of green. We were desperate to swim on hot summer days, so my mother sent Yael and I for lessons with Mrs. Van der Merwe at the Borrow Street swimming pool. My mother said Mrs. Van had been an Olympic diver and that we were lucky to have such an incredible person to teach us to swim. Mrs. Van's deeply tanned skin gave her a leathery look. Her cropped hair was speckled with streaks of brown, orange and yellow. At my first lesson, I was told to hold onto a plank of wood, on one end of which was a long piece of rope. Holding the rope in one hand, Mrs. Van picked me up and shouted "hold tight and shut your mouth" into my ear. Then she threw me into the pool like a bag of potatoes and set off at a steady pace along the side of the pool. I sailed along on the end of her rope, swallowing gallons of water as I went. After a few lessons, she dropped the rope into the water and shouted, "kick your bladdy socks off", then left me to power my way aimlessly around the pool, until she blew her whistle. After a few more lessons, she decided the time had come to snatch the wood out of my hands. Everything I'd learned suddenly came into focus. Over those agonising weeks, I would look up at Yael in his Speedo swimming costume as he waited for his turn. He stood with his fingers in his ears as I splashed and cried my way around the pool. His turn soon came to be thrown into the water, clutching on to his piece of wood, and he too learned "to kick his bladdy socks off" in no time at all.

Mrs. Van der Merwe and her swimming lessons pale into insignificance when I think of all the fun that we had in the Baxter's swimming tank. We spent hours climbing up on to the side and throwing ourselves into the water. The joy of swimming turned even our bath times into fun times. One evening, Yael was rolling around on top of me in the bath, when my father rushed in, pulled him off and smacked him very hard on the bottom. Then he hauled me out and hit me too, as hard as he could. He shouted at us and then disappeared. He clearly thought we were having sex in the bath but was too enraged or embarrassed to ask us what we were doing. He was not to know we were playing at being whales just as we did in the Baxter's tank.

Part Two

Seven

My mother wrote: *"The Baxters came about 1963. They were a mixed religion family. Hazel took the kids to Mass (Roman Catholic) and Paddy was a Church of England person. Hazel played tennis and was really keen, so she pressed me to allow you to go to classes with Colonel Collins at Suburbs on Saturday afternoon. I thought you were too young but said "Yes" and hoped for you to decide. To my delight you enjoyed playing. Colonel and Mrs Collins thought you had a natural talent and so we were happy. Lionel willingly paid for coaching for you, Elaine and subsequently Yael. Justine was not at all interested in sport."*

Hazel made us a pair of matching tennis dresses. My dress was sleeveless, with a round necked bodice, a low waist and a gathered skirt. She made a pocket above the skirt, just roomy enough to hold a tennis ball. The waist and pocket were edged with a thin ribbon which had blue, red and green flowers embroidered on it. I loved the way my dress swung around my hips as well as the blue and white frilly knickers she made to go underneath. My mother bought me a Maxply tennis racquet which smelled like her clear nail polish. She said the strings were yellow because they were made of cat gut. Its red leather grip had a rich animal smell.

Our tennis teacher, Colonel Ray Collins was a retired British army officer. He was a tall man with clear blue eyes and a bushy moustache. His arms and legs were tanned a deep nut brown against his white shorts. He wore white takkies, white socks with blue stripes at the top and a white shirt. Even when the sun made the sand on the tennis court shimmer with heat, and the cicadas sang like alarm bells, the Colonel wore his creamy woollen pullover with its cable patterns and the badge on it which said 'Fred Perry'. He wore a battered old khaki hat, his eyes hidden behind dark glasses. He stood next to the net, holding himself in an erect and commanding pose. Ray had played county tennis before the war and he said we all had the potential to play in the Wimbledon Tennis Championships, if we obeyed his instructions. He wore an enormous gold ring on his little finger. He didn't sound anything like my father, but he and my mother developed a strong and lasting friendship. She got involved in managing one of the provincial tennis teams as we grew older.

Penny and I skidded around on the sandy court while the Colonel told us how to hold our racquets and when to swing at the ball. He would often walk over to hold an arm and demonstrate the way to swing, adjust a grip or position a foot. We watched in awe as he hit a ball over the net with effortless accuracy and we gazed in wonder at the power of his serves. He could smash balls with precision and then amble up to the net like a graceful giraffe. He volleyed back the balls we hit at him with an air of nonchalance.

Ray used an electric machine which made a rattling noise like a machine gun. It had a firing arm which hit balls over the net at different speeds. The machine had a wire basket at the top and as each ball was fired, another dropped into position. The arm was fitted to an enormous metal spring which had to be adjusted manually. The Colonel employed two young Africans, Willard and Maxim to operate the machine. The exertion of doing so made the muscles in their arms and legs bulge as they strained to follow the Colonel's orders. They man-handled the machine on its iron wheels, pushing it at angles as instructed. Maxim was a bit younger than Willard and I remember he fired the machine with more precision and force than Willard did.

Over the years the Colonel taught them to play tennis. Maxim's serves made the ball zing past our ears to embed itself in the fence behind us. Willard was much kinder when he played with us and he listened to the Colonel's rules about being a good sport and a gentleman. Willard wore the same kind of khaki hat as Ray and he too had a chunky gold ring on his little finger. As the years went by

Willard regularly played games against us. Although he became an expert tennis player, he wasn't permitted to be a member at the tennis club where the Colonel held his classes because black people were segregated from every aspect of white society. He and Maxim took turns at collecting the balls around the court and they helped each other load up the machine for the next round of shots.

Ray's wife Annabel came along to our lessons and sat next to the net in a deck chair. She was a tiny woman with grey wispy hair hidden under the brim of her sun hat. My mother said Annabel was very quiet because she had lost both her children in the war. She clicked her tongue when she told us and said Annabel sipped gin out of her thermos flask because you didn't ever get over a thing like that. Annabel used to let Penny and I stroke the mouse brooch she'd pinned on the front of her hat. She said it was special because it was made out of mink fur. Her red lipstick was smudged on her front teeth. When my mother told me about the gin, I realised it was Annabel's breath which stank and not her mousey brooch.

While we waited for our mothers to collect us, we sipped orange juice out of paper cups. Ray poured himself a cup of tea out of his thermos. He would then eat his sandwiches and give us a talk about tactics. Still munching his sandwiches, the morning lesson ended with the presentation ceremony. Every week it was possible for one of us to win a gold badge. The winner was the person who had the highest score of balls over the net and into court. Ten badges added up to a gold tie pin. Ten gold tie pins earned a match, the best of three games, against the Colonel himself. He seldom lost a point, but when he did, he always said the same thing: "Keep that up and I'll be watching you hold the Wimbledon Singles Trophy above your head one day." Willard and Maxim re-painted the lines on the court while the presentation took place. They mixed up the whitewash in a tin can with a stick and then poured it into a machine on wheels. They pulled pieces of string into straight lines and hammered them in place. The machine dispensed paint as it was pushed along on its little wheels. It had the same fresh smell as the whitewash our servants used to paint onto my takkies to keep them looking new.

I practised my tennis strokes against the back of the servants' quarters. I smashed tennis balls from the top lawn to the bottom lawn, hitting them so hard and high they sailed over the house and into the fruit orchard behind the kitchen. I bounced a ball up and down on the strings until I lost count. I practised flicking my racquet out of my hand and catching it on the handle like I'd seen the cowboys in Bonanza doing with their guns. After a while, Ray told my mother I was showing promise and suggested I started having private lessons with him. So, I went along for an hour before the group lesson, when there was not another soul at the Suburbs Tennis Club, and I had the Colonel and his machine to myself.

I won the Matabeleland Under Twelve Girls Singles in 1966. The Colonel pronounced me "Queen Victoria of the tennis court". I was chosen to play for Matabeleland when I was thirteen. The Bulawayo Chronicle ran a story with the heading: "Little Charlie saves Face for Matabeleland". I remember staring at my name and photograph in the newspaper with a mixture of disbelief and pleasure. My father said I must be careful not to let it go to my head. Yael started having lessons with the Colonel too and soon we were hitting tennis balls at each other as well as playing war games around the garden armed with mudballs.

Penny's enthusiasm for tennis was not as great as mine so we often went off on our bikes to play amongst the tomato plants at the hospital farm. When Yael was with us, we threw rotten ones at each other and played hide and seek in the disused barns.

Penny and I were allowed to cycle over to an old quarry near the St. Francis Home. We left our bikes at the top and slid our way down its sandy sides on our bottoms. We never dared swim in the stagnant water because my father said we'd get sleeping sickness from bilharzia. One day, when we were skimming stones at the water's edge, a movement on the edge of the quarry caught my eye and I saw a group of Africans ducking and diving their way through the tall grasses. One of them caught sight of us and signalled me to be quiet. Then their silhouettes peered down at us and I grabbed Penny by the arm. We scuttled out of sight and hid ourselves away. We stayed there for a long time before we found the courage to make a run for it and scamper back up to the top. We grabbed our bikes and pedalled home as fast as we could. In our panic we were not sure who or what we had seen. I told Penny they must have been Red Indians and Penny said she was pretty sure they were leprechauns. We agreed not to tell our parents and it took us a while before we felt brave enough to play at the quarry once more. After Penny and her family moved away, I never went to the quarry again.

Years later, when I was researching the history of the hospital, I discovered that inmates often escaped by running away through the seven hundred acres of grassland that surrounded the hospital buildings. We'd seen a group of people making their way to freedom.

Eight

Yael remembers he and I went swimming at the Baxter's house the day before Paddy died. He wrote: *"I remember swimming with you in the Baxter's pool on the Saturday. Paddy Baxter was with us in the pool. On Sunday afternoon, Lionel took me to the boating pond in the Bulawayo park to make me feel better. That is all I remember."* It was a sweltering afternoon when Yael and I went next door for a swim. I carried on swimming after Paddy got out of the pool and Yael went back home. I jumped off the side of the tank onto Penny's lilo. It let out a hiss and sank into the choppy water of the pool. I was afraid I'd broken it and was sure I'd get into trouble. So, I stayed bobbing up and down, too afraid to take the useless lilo to Paddy and explain what had happened. It is sad thinking back to that day, that I was too embarrassed to go and say goodbye. I never saw Paddy or any of his family again.

I wrote and asked my mother to tell me what she remembered about Paddy's death. She wrote: *"The Baxters were a strange crowd – the children were very disturbed by the religious teaching. I remember Penny frightening you with stories of purgatory and being "in limbo" if you died without being in a "state of grace".*

As for Paddy's death you and Yael went swimming on Sat p.m. and I had invited Paddy for lunch on the following day. Hazel and the kids were in Cape Town with her mother and he was alone over Christmas and New Year. On Sunday a.m. I told our servants Paddy would be here for lunch and what to make etc. and went to have a bath. Their servant came up to say she could not find Paddy and I told her to look for the car because he was probably in one of the wards. I said I would come over, so I got out of the bath, dressed and walked over. As I came near to the Little House, I smelt ether. I remember being anxious and walked into the house through the back door. I called and walked to the main bedroom. The bed had been slept in and the light was on – unusual because it was light. Then I knocked on the bathroom door and it was locked. I went outside to try to see through the window. By now I was really worried, so I tried to find Lionel on the ward, and by great luck, I found him talking to Dennis Peterson (a senior doctor in Rhodesia – President of the Medical Council). I told Lionel the situation and asked them both to come over. I phoned Elaine and asked her to restrain you and Yael from coming over because I didn't want you two to come and find the Police, etc. Anyway, eventually the Police broke the window and Paddy was dead in the bath, with a plastic bag over his head. Dr. Montgomery explained that Paddy had been with them for dinner on Saturday night and they had discussed a theory that certain patients' psychoses were eased by causing brief unconsciousness with the use of ether on patients. So, no-one could decide if Paddy's death was accidental or a suicide.

I remember coming back to our house and dear Elaine sat me down, made me tea, made me toast and she comforted me because I was very upset by this event, and dreaded Hazel's return and reactions. However, all was well. Hazel took herself back to Cape Town and the children stayed with their grandmother. Eventually, she married Rupert and so far as I know, they now all live in South Africa. The little house was occupied by the Chief Nursing Officer after that. We did not tell you or Yael about suicide, etc but that Paddy had had a heart attack and you both shed a few tears. That's all I can tell you."

Paddy died on Sunday 3rd January 1965. I still have two precious books which Penny gave me: *A Friend is Someone Who Likes You* and *A Pocketful of Proverbs* by Joan Walsh Anglund. They are miniature books with a line drawing on every page. *A Pocketful of Proverbs* slips inside a hard cover pocket with a patchwork design on it. On the back, in red letters, I wrote: "Charlotte Perelman. Given to me by Penny 20.7.66". Hazel gave me *A Pocketful of Proverbs* when she came to Bulawayo for the inquest into Paddy's death. When I look at the books, I see it was not so much the words that appealed to me but the lovely pen and ink illustrations of children. Losing the Baxters, especially Penny, was a terrible blow.

The date on the back of *A Pocketful of Proverbs* is significant because it's the day after my eleventh birthday. I remember my mother gave the book to me some time before my birthday when I was ill in bed. My father said I had the measles and I remember my mother laughing and saying it was a fateful date because it was 6.6.66. It was the only time I got to sleep all night in my parents' bed. I remember having hallucinations and seeing little green men running all over the eiderdown. My mother sat next to me with a bowl of iced water and sponged my forehead with icy bits of cotton wool. She gave me *A Pocketful of Proverbs* to help me feel better. I wrote the inscription after having another birthday without Penny there to share it with me.

Nine

Mrs. Coetzee's house was on Lobengula Street. My mother took me there to have my tennis dresses made after the Baxters moved away. Jacoba Coetzee was the seamstress at the hospital. She was an Afrikaner woman whose nose looked like a purple carbuncle. She took my measurements with a filthy tape measure and a cigarette dangled out of her mouth as she spoke. Old Coetz smelled of alcohol and the bruises on her face matched the colour of her nose.

On 11th November 1965, the Prime Minister of Rhodesia, Ian Douglas Smith declared Unilateral Independence (UDI) from Great Britain. It is possible to listen again to Smith speaking on the Rhodesian Broadcasting Corporation website. Smith had been a fighter pilot with the Royal Air Force during World War Two. He suffered terrible injuries as a result of being shot down over enemy territory. Smith had a slurpy way of speaking: "We, the Europeans, we are all powerful. We have the reins in our hands, and we can pretty much do what we like." My father sat on the Mental Health Board of Rhodesia. He had connections with the judiciary and the Chief Commissioner of the British South Africa Police, so he had a firm grip on the reins of power.

My mother told me about UDI as we drove home one day from school. She said it meant no more chocolates or cigarettes because Great Britain had imposed sanctions against us. The Rhodesians invented a brand of chocolates called Charons and cigarettes in a pale blue box called Kingsgate. Both brought mutterings from my parents about having to put up with lower standards. My father shook his head about the growing "communist threat" and he said, "the terrorists had support in the Tribal Trust Lands and were causing bladdy carnage". He said, "good old Smithy would sort out the bladdy kaffirs once and for all". There were programmes on the radio for 'our boys in the bush', defending the country out in the sweltering grassland where not only 'gooks' lurked but wild animals too. Daniel Carney wrote a book called *The Whispering Death* about an albino terrorist who was tracked down and killed by a captain in the Selous Scouts. A brutal showdown in a dry riverbed gave me nightmares for weeks after I read it.

I rode my bike over to the Bradfield shops where I would spend hours flipping through picture books with photographs of soldiers armed with AK 47's. There were pictures of dead men, women and children, their throats cut and their bodies lying in black pools of blood. There were photos of bullet riddled cars with dead Europeans slumped half out of open doors, with blood dripping down their lifeless faces. The soldiers were hunting the terrorist killers.

After UDI nobody stood to attention in the cinema when the British National Anthem was played. When my mother took me and my sisters to see "The Sound of Music", I obediently rose out of my seat as "God Save the

Queen" began to play. Somebody had forgotten to edit the film after Smith's momentous declaration, and I was roughly tugged back down by someone seated behind me. Justine glared at me and my mother shifted uncomfortably in her seat.

Towards the end of 1965, a new hall was built at the hospital. I wore my blue silk dress with silver smocking across the top to attend the opening concert with my parents. I sat cross-legged on the floor with some of the other children. Mr Radcliffe came over with a microphone and knelt down beside me. He asked me to sing Eidelweiss with him. I knew it came from The Sound of Music, but I didn't know any of the words. I wished the floor would swallow me up because Mr Radcliffe stayed and sang the whole thing with me sitting on his knee.

I later found out that George Radcliffe was accused of sexually molesting a boy on one of the wards, but no charges were pressed by the superintendent.

Yael remembers the day Elaine left home more clearly than I do. He recalls we went for a farewell meal at the Southern Sun Hotel where he and I shared a smoked salmon starter. He said he and Elaine sipped champagne with Justine and my parents. We drove to the station in two cars so we could all say goodbye to her. Yael remembers he, my father and Elaine walked to the luggage car where they stowed away the grey suitcases, with leather patches on the corners that my mother had bought at Haddon and Sly. I remember my nineteen-year-old sister looking out from the carriage window as we waited for the guard to blow his whistle. The train took her to Cape Town, where she boarded the Edinburgh Castle and sailed to Southampton. She journeyed on by train to take up her place at Durham University.

In 1970, Elaine donated the money my mother had siphoned into a savings account to the Peruvian earthquake disaster fund. I remember telling my friends at school what a great humanitarian thing my sister did. My parents were stunned.

When I went on holiday to England in 1978, the bespectacled dark-haired woman who came to meet me one hot summer's day was a complete stranger. I had knitted Elaine a winter scarf in anticipation of meeting her again, but it didn't warm the thirteen years that stretched between us like a tightrope. As she walked me and my heavy suitcase to her flat, I sweated in my brown tweed trouser suit and struggled to know what to say. Elaine was so utterly different from Justine that I felt at sea with her. It didn't help that her flatmates were French speakers.

Elaine and I grew closer when I came to live in England many years later. She has become my mentor and a cherished friend.

In 1966 my mother got a fancy new car; it was a pale green Citroen shaped a bit like a frog. Its power steering made handling the car an effortless exercise. Its hydraulic brakes sighed as it glided to a halt. The car rose up and floated on a bed of air when the driver pulled up a lever on the floor underneath the seat. We rose along with the car as it transformed itself into a magic carpet on wheels. We sailed gracefully over the enormous humps across Bulawayo's wide streets. The humps were built to prevent flooding in the city centre during thunderstorms, when gallons of water fell from the sky in a matter of minutes.

When Yael and I learned to drive, we used to aquaplane in my father's white Mini through the miniature lakes which grew on either side of the humps.

Yael's driving instructor warned him to "watch out for jungle bunnies" pointing to African pedestrians who were allowed to work in the industrial areas where he took Yael to practise. His instructor would wind down his window and shout "It's no bloody good having road signs in this country is it? It's time you kaffirs learned to read so you know who's got the right of way!"

Yael and I often pedalled over to the hospital farm - past the female ward, along the crunchy cinder track until we came to the fields where the barns and the old cattle sheds stood empty. Pungent with smells, clouds of flies buzzed around clods of old manure and bits of hay drifted in the hot air. Fine spray from the sprinklers which spat in the distance gave us snatches of relief from the heat. I loved that peaceful other world where row upon row of green things stretched as far as the eye could see into the distance.

Tomatoes, spinach, potatoes and mealies grew in abundance. Sometimes we saw inmates toiling in the fields amongst the crops. Guards stood around with their knobkerries dangling off their belts. Their polished boots glistened in the sun. They wore their khaki hats with leather straps under their chins to keep the sun off their heads. The farm tractor and its trailer waited to ferry the men and the things they picked back to the hospital storerooms.

More often than not we found the farm deserted. Then we would chase each other across the fields. We would throw mud balls, and tomatoes, and whatever else was close to hand at each other.

I loved the sweet aroma which leaked out of the papery covers around ripening mealies. The yellow corn inside its hairy outer cocoon lay incubating like an exotic treasure. The stringy tangle of hairs brought with it the sensual pleasure of unwrapping something forbidden and sweet-smelling.

Ten

As tournaments became the focus of our school holidays, Yael and I began to play tennis further afield. This gave us a chance to stay with other families. We loved staying with the Frobishers who lived in Salisbury because they had a swimming pool carved out of a granite boulder, as well as an all-weather tennis court. There was a thatched summer house next to the tennis court where Dr. Frobisher kept a brass trumpet. When their daughter Annabel, known as Binks, wanted to summon the servants to bring us some refreshments, she got the trumpet and blew it. Their pool had a bar in the middle of it where Dr. and Mrs. Frobisher entertained friends. Gwen Frobisher took us to the tennis tournament in her red Ford Capri which had rounded windows in the back. Yael and I pretended we were sitting in an aeroplane. Binks, sitting next to her mother, was the co-pilot. Yael and I sat in the back and sipped our imaginary drinks while we puffed on our imaginary cigarettes.

I met up again with the Frobishers in 1986. I asked them what happened to Dolly and Sixpence who used to wait on us when we stayed with them. Dolly and Sixpence had continued to keep house in post-independent Zimbabwe, after the Frobishers returned to live in England. Sixpence was always immaculate in his starched white trousers and scarlet jacket. The jacket was edged with gold braid and he wore a red hat like a fez. The gold tassel on top of his hat was the same as the gold tassel on the end of the bell pull in the dining room. Mrs. Frobisher said they'd decided it was time for Sixpence to retire when he turned sixty, so they'd flown him to Cape Town in their private jet for a farewell ceremony. They gave him a sum of money rather than getting him some cattle and had then flown him back to Harare. She said Sixpence drank so much when he returned to his village that he died soon afterwards. I remember telling my mother what had happened, and my father said, "Once a muntu always a muntu."

Our servants complained about the amount of time I spent hitting balls against the back of their quarters. I'd overheard the Colonel saying that I was showing enough promise to play at Wimbledon, so I redoubled my efforts. I constantly nagged Yael to play tennis with me. I hit tennis balls over the house, bounced balls to strengthen my wrist and broke the kitchen window. After I was told to stop hitting balls anywhere near the house, I took all the eggs out of the pantry. I threw the eggs, one after the other, against the wall behind the servants' quarters. I frog-marched Yael to the scene of my crime and pinned him to the wall. My mother caught me making him stand to attention against the wall while I squashed the last remaining egg on his head.

My mother eventually persuaded my father to get the Public Works Department to fix up the clay tennis court at our house. At first, Yael was as enthusiastic about playing tennis as I was, and we began to spend hours playing games against each other and practising our strokes. It became a sore point, however, when Yael began to use the tennis court as a landing strip for his model aeroplane. He and my father would carry the plane and a flagon of fuel onto the court. There they would fill up its tank with evil smelling petrol. My father twiddled the propeller around while Yael stood clutching the end of a long rope. My father would kneel down and brace himself to release it, making sure not to have his fingers reduced to mincemeat in its whirling propeller. They would wait for its engine to reach fever pitch, before my father jumped out the way and the plane would race off at the end of its rope. Yael would whirl himself around keeping his eyes fixed on the screeching thing, watching for it to lift itself off the ground. It would rise magnificently into the air and Yael became a whirling dervish as it roared above his head. It didn't take long before it would spin out of control and crash, gouging holes along the surface of my beloved tennis court. My father never once saw me hit a tennis ball although he reported my successes to Miss Garth the matron and his secretary Mrs. Grey.

Yael's willingness to play tennis with me began to wane. I remember his look of resignation on those hot afternoons, when he threw his racquet to one side and walked stoically over to net. When I had hit him three times at close range, he sauntered off into the coolness of the house while I continued to batter balls against the wire fence around the court. My mother took pity on Yael and soon the Public Works Department built a practice wall along one end of the court. Now I smashed my way through one hot afternoon after another. As I began to win more tournaments, I got a sponsorship deal with Maxply. My mother collected my new racquets from the sports department in Miekles and brought them home in thick plastic covers, smelling of leather and varnish. Prior to a tennis match, I slept with my right arm in a fixed position so it wouldn't be stiff in the morning. Before my matches I said a prayer. I said prayers before I got into bed and I said prayers when I touched the gold St. Christopher around my neck that Penny gave me. I gave my St. Christopher a kiss before delivering a serve which needed to be an ace. I said prayers when I was about to lose.

When my father got in from work and my mother told him I'd won, he said "good old Champ. Don't go getting big-headed over it".

Eleven

Yael and I used to race our bikes up and down the long driveway. One afternoon he had a hideous accident and had to be rushed to hospital. He wrote: *"I cut my leg open when I was in Form One. I must have been around twelve or thirteen. It was Shareen who rode in front of me – we were playing with her and her brother. The accident wasn't her fault nor anyone else's. The consequences could have been dire for me but thankfully weren't."* The brake on Yael's bike impaled itself in the top of his thigh and ripped his leg open in a spectacular way. I remember looking in shock at a black blood vessel throbbing at the bottom of the wound and feeling sick. My mother rushed him to hospital, and he came home with lots of tiny black stitches in his leg. Yael said the doctor told him just a millimetre either way and he would have bled to death. I used to look at the fat scar on his leg with awe. I felt a massive sense of relief to find out it hadn't been my fault. Justine remembered the accident too: *"As Yael says, we all got hammered at various times and the only clear memory of a specific incident that I have, is when Yael cut his leg and was in so much pain that Lionel told him if he didn't stop crying, he'd give him something to cry about – I've never forgotten how cross I was and it still makes me feel sad."*

It's been sad to remember how often my father lashed out at us. Yael wrote: *"Charlotte, we got smacked fairly often, which was 'normal' in those days. You frequently set me up for it! I remember crying about something – Lionel gave me a smash on the bottom and said, "that'll give you something to cry about". The worst incident was when you chucked a mud ball at me. I was running and by a complete fluke you hit me. Luckily it hit me on the side of my head and missed my eye. Kids do these things. Do you remember when we threw squibs at Shareen? If any of those had hit her in the face she could have been blinded or disfigured. Thankfully they didn't!"* I also remember how Yael graciously told my parents he'd accidentally run into a tree to save me from being punished.

The time he fell over the bridge at the bottom of the drive and gashed his head open was another awful memory. He wrote: *"You didn't push me off the little bridge – I fell off because I was showing off. I remember holding my feet and arms in the air and leaning the bike against the bridge and shouting, "look at me". With nothing to support the bike it toppled over and I fell over the bridge. I didn't hurt myself badly."* I felt sad that Yael regarded a wound which needed stitching and left a noticeable scar on his forehead to be a minor injury. It was a substantial drop onto solid concrete, and he had landed on his head after all. It was a relief to know I wasn't responsible for that accident either.

We used to tease one another mercilessly. Justine's pointy nails came in useful for pinching and pummelling the two of us when we annoyed her. On one occasion, she kicked me and caught my ankle bone, thus breaking her big toe. She used to moan bitterly about my leaving pubic hairs in the bath and on the soap. There was a time when she wouldn't use the bathroom until I had plucked them out of the soap, changed the towels and cleaned the bath. I never considered that they might be hers!

Justine wrote: *"If anything I tried to ignore Susan and Lionel for most of my teens and hoped they'd do the same to me as I wasn't good at anything particularly except talking to my friends, smoking a lot and having fun. I do remember once when I'd cut my head open from throwing rocks at the water cooler, Lionel didn't think I should take any more codeine, even though I had a dreadful headache. I had a seizure caused by taking anorexine, which was extremely naughty and careless at that age. I wanted to be thinner and anorexine was an amphetamine that killed the appetite and gave one lots of energy. Of course, I never told anyone about that, but Derek knew. So, I don't think I was brain damaged at birth as Lionel told you I was, nor was I epileptic; just didn't have the courage to own up to what I'd done! I had all kinds of EEG's at the Bulawayo General and was never found to have any sign of epilepsy – the stupid things we do!"*

I started attending Townsend High School in 1967. It was a single-sex school with an impressive range of sports facilities and well-tended grounds. Many girls at Townsend came from farming and mining families and were full-time boarders. Two of my classmates became outstanding athletes who represented the country at the Junior Olympics. My parents were pleased that I was put into the A stream like Elaine, and not the C stream like Justine. The streaming system included an R class for girls who struggled with academic subjects. The R stood for Remove.

Yael and I remember 1969 as a momentous year. My mother went into hospital to have surgery on her throat. Yael wrote: *"She had a lump removed from her neck – the lump has a name which I can't recall. I think it was a goitre??"* When she came out of hospital, she showed us the delicate scar at the bottom of her throat. She said how grateful she was that her surgeon made the incision exactly on her necklace line, so nobody would notice her scar. I remember one day, shortly after she came home from the hospital, we were standing in the rose garden and she pointed out a flock of geese flying in formation overhead. She said "Just before I was put under the anaesthetic, I looked out of the window and saw a flock of birds just like that. I wondered if that was the last thing I would ever see." She looked at me and said: "It's easy to die, you know Charlotte!" I remember the ground under my feet wobbled and the scar just below her Adam's apple took on a new significance.

When she'd recovered from the operation, my mother took Justine with her to visit Elaine in England. Elaine's academic achievements were highly regarded in our family. Justine, with her passion for partying, trendy clothes and glamourous hairstyles caused my father consternation but gained my mother's interest. I existed somewhere in between, tormenting Yael and smashing tennis balls against walls. Thankfully my sporting achievements gave me a way of fitting in at school.

My mother and Justine began their trip with a visit to Barbara who still lived next door to Susan's family home. Elaine met them at Barbara's, and they spent a week travelling together. Then Susan took Justine to meet old friends from her time as a student nurse at University College Hospital. They travelled on to Switzerland, followed by a visit to Lake Como. When I looked at the photographs of their trip, I barely recognised Elaine. With a cigarette in one hand, her hair cropped short and wearing black-rimmed glasses she looked more like Bob Dylan than my sister. My mother bought me back a Swiss tennis cap. She said it made me look like Suzanne Lenglen. I only wore it once for the photograph she took because it was a size too small.

While they were away, I was admitted to the Mater Dei Hospital to have my appendix removed. The thing I remember most was being given a pre-med capsule to swallow by one of the nursing Sisters. She was also a nun, and reminded me of the Sisters at St. Francis. The nurse said the pill would make me feel drowsy before they took me to the operating theatre. I had never swallowed a pill before, and I bit it in half. The medicine inside it was foul but I gamely swallowed it down. I spent some weeks in the Mater Dei being nursed back to health by the Sisters. My father came to visit, and a number of my mother's friends stopped by with magazines and games to keep me occupied. I came out of hospital a few days before my mother and Justine got back.

It wasn't long before our family life went back to normal, Yael and I resuming our mud-ball fights and skirmishes on the tennis court once more.

Twelve

One glorious summer, Justine's best friend Bethany O'Malley invited me and Yael to come over and swim. Bethany lived within walking distance of the hospital. Her parents were friendly and said we could go over to her house and swim whether Bethany was there or not. So, whenever our hearts desired, we tucked our swimming things under our arms and ran through the waving grasses, over the burning soil, as fast as our legs could carry us. All the kids in the neighbour-hood had an open invitation to swim there. Gone were the days of having to jump in the fishpond to cool off and risk the sinister toad we named Sweet Pea who lurked in its depths. No more having to run around in the sprinkler on the top lawn. Gone were the weekends of being stuck in the house with nothing to do except play tennis or ride our bikes. We swam in the O'Malley's pool for hours and hours and hours. We ran back home bedraggled and tired, our eyes red and hazy from keeping them open underwater.

When I wasn't at school or underwater in the O'Malley's pool, I was playing tennis. Life became simple and I regularly fell in and out of love. I danced long and slow one night with a dark-haired boy who offered to drive me back to the hospital. We stood and kissed in the moonlight. I showed him the Queen of the Night which grew near the car port. Its multitude of white petals glowed, pale and ethereal under the stars. For months afterwards I pined after him like a dog without a bone. He never invited me out or spoke to me again. I wondered if his parents were upset that he'd fallen in love with a girl who lived at the local lunatic asylum. Besides, I wasn't properly Jewish so I'm sure his family weren't keen on allowing our romance to blossom. I had to accept that the dark-haired boy was not to be mine.

I tried not to look Jewish. I tried sleeping with an elastic band stretched around the back of my head and underneath my nose so that it might point skywards. Despite doing this for months, my nose stayed as it was. It was only as an adult that I realised it was not so much my Jewish looks that made me so different, but my home on Twenty-Third Avenue. This was known to everyone in town as the road which led into the grounds of Ingutsheni, a place where parents could send children who were behaving badly. My success as a tennis player helped me fit in at school.

Justine met Derek Williams shortly before her 21st birthday. I climbed out of my bedroom window so I could spy on the guests at her party. With a certain amount of satisfaction, I watched Derek and some of his friends take a communal piss in the fishpond. Derek intoned the words "dominus rectum" in a loud and serious way as they all urinated into the water. I watched Justine stride over to reprimand him. "The Mother Superior's never going to know" he laughed in his high-pitched way.

Much to my father's chagrin, Derek became a regular visitor. Derek, he said, was an alcoholic and a cradle-snatcher, being fifteen years older than Justine, and the father of two grown-up children. Derek sold expensive men's clothing. He wore a chunky gold necklace which dangled down his hairy chest and a thick gold ring on a little finger. He was a freckled Warren Beatty who dressed as suavely as James Bond.

Derek's driver Johnson wore a grey uniform with a peaked cap. He used the same generous application of Brut deodorant as Derek did. He kept a clipper in his top pocket so he could trim Derek's cigars. Derek said Johnson was 'not only the best looking but also the best smelling zot around'.

I was thrilled to be invited to play squash against him at the Parkview Sports Club. I wasn't able to win more than a few points, but I didn't care. Afterwards, I sat next to him and Justine at the bar while they sipped their drinks, smoked their cigars and introduced me to Bulawayo's other 'beautiful people'.

When Derek developed a cancerous growth on his tongue, he was subjected to a lengthy course of treatment in the Bulawayo General Hospital. I cringed at the thought of him having to have radium needles stuck into his tongue. Justine spent every spare moment at his bedside in the hospital. Cigars were banned for a long time afterwards and he eventually made a full recovery. From that point onwards he and Justine became inseparable.

The 'mother superior' developed a soft spot for Derek which would last for the rest of her life.

Thirteen

We moved away from the hospital in 1971 to live in a four-bedroomed bungalow in a residential area known as Suburbs, a short bicycle ride away from the city centre. I had just turned sixteen and was about to write my O Levels. Justine and I shared a brand-new bathroom and Justine's bedroom had an outside door. Our section of the house was decorated in shades of pink, white, black and turquoise. I had a new iron bed with gold knobs on either end, and Justine had a glamorous pink paisley eiderdown. It was amazing to be able to ride over to the Centenary Park and to visit Bulawayo's beautiful Natural History Museum whenever I wanted. I spent many contented hours in the museum, admiring its collection of stuffed lions, zebra, antelope, warthogs and mighty elephants. I loved the displays of butterflies, beetles and birds. I could ride my bike to Townsend High School ten minutes away along suburban roads. There were streetlights outside my window and classmates around the corner.

The servants' two tiny rooms were next to a triple car shelter at the back of the house. My mother drove her Citroen up a paved driveway round the back of the house to the kitchen where the servants unloaded her shopping bags. Justine had been given a pale blue Anglia for her twenty first birthday. She was able to park outside her bedroom and let herself in and out of her private annexe without disturbing the rest of us.

Lionel went into private practice in a block of offices near the Bulawayo Public Library. Now everyone, except my mother, lay in a row on sun beds around the sparkling new swimming pool, roasting under the sun.

When I got my driving licence in 1972, I was allowed to use Justine's car to go and buy her an ice cream from the Eskimo Hut ice cream parlour near the Bulawayo Fair Grounds. She gave me enough money for a tub of vanilla ice cream smothered in chocolate sauce for her, myself and Yael. Yael was always keen to come and hold Justine's ice cream on his lap while he spooned his into his mouth. When we got home, Justine devoured hers to save it from melting. Then we fell into the clear blue water of the pool, swam, sunbathed and swam some more, until our servant Martha rang the bell for supper.

As part of my A Level studies, my geography class went on an expedition to the Mushandike Study Centre near Fort Nicholson for a long weekend. I had a tremendous fight with my mother prior to our departure because I'd fallen in love with Freddie Compton during a tennis tournament in Salisbury. Freddie was to be in Bulawayo that weekend as a member of his school hockey team. There is a photograph of us girls arriving at the camp, with me standing to one side, glowering sulkily at the camera. However, my sourness soon lifted when I realised two young game rangers were to be our hosts for the week. They took us giggling schoolgirls potholing in caves infested with bat dung, canoeing on dams rich in bird life, particularly fish eagles, and, armed with rifles, into the countryside to track wild animals. I came home with stories of barbeques and sun downers as well as rapturous feelings for Kev and Ollie. The escalating war had not featured on my radar at all. This was 1972 and the liberation struggle for Independence was well under way. Yael was fifteen and not yet eligible for compulsory military service at eighteen.

Not long after I got back, my father told me the school had been in touch with him to complain about my behaviour. He said if it wasn't for him, I would have been expelled by the headmistress for being drunk and disorderly at the barbeque we'd had on the last night. In the aftermath, I took to my bed and said I couldn't face going to school. My father said I'd learned an important lesson about decency and the consequences of alcohol poisoning. My mother kept me off school while I underwent a series of blood and urine tests. Every evening when my father got home, he would poke his head around the door into my bedroom and say, "How's sicky today?" I missed so much school that I failed to take my matriculation exams. This meant that I had to pass all three of my A Level subjects to go and study at university.

Part Two

Fourteen

I began my degree in 1974 at the University of Cape Town. I met Gordon towards the end of my first year. For our autumn vacation, Gordon borrowed his father's car and we drove along the Garden Route to visit my friend Mel, who was studying social work at Rhodes University in Grahamstown.

Mel and I are still in touch. She wrote: *"My experience with Ingutsheni would have been around 1978-1980, so just pre-Independence. What I remember is that most people seemed to be on Largactil with its resulting tanned yellow skin look! I have a memory of a young woman walking down along the veranda and then lying down and lifting her dress .... So distressing. I was told that their primal urges are very strong, and they engaged in sexual acts often. I think I possibly met with the super on one occasion to discuss a patient, and I was fairly impressed with the diagnosis and understanding of the patient (he was black and I think witchcraft was taken into account) but it was a very medical approach with medication playing a large part. My other experience was social: my friend Gillian worked there, and she used to get us all involved every now and then usually on a Saturday night for the patient's social evening. We would pitch up in this hall and see epileptic patients with helmets on their heads and be grabbed by patients who would drive us round the hall in a kind of dance. One patient insisted on tying our shoelaces. We found it a strange mix of humour, pathos and gut-wrenching compassion."*

Justine wrote: *"I remember how angry Lionel was about Dr. Montgomery and the helmets he invented for those poor people with epilepsy. It wasn't even to do with it being inappropriate. Lionel was angry that Montgomery was getting extra income out of those stupid helmets."*

I quit my degree towards the end of 1975. Justine collected me at the airport, and I was thrilled to be back home, ready to begin a secretarial course at Speciss College. My father said I had 'screwed up my life' and shunned me. This took me by surprise because I'd obeyed his orders and had been to see a psychiatrist in Cape Town to talk over my decision to give up my studies. The psychiatrist had been very supportive and said that I clearly knew my own mind. I avoided my father as much as I could and went to college in the morning, worked in the afternoons as a teacher's assistant at the Athol Desmond Study Centre, and took a job as a waitress at the Holiday Inn in the evenings. My father refused to accept my decision and so I paid for the course myself.

At the study centre, I became friends with Alfred Mpofu who worked there as a cleaner. Alfred was studying English in his spare time. I remember telling Alfred about Franco Zefferelli's film of Romeo and Juliet, which was showing at the time. Alfred pointed out that he wasn't allowed into the cinema. During our tea break, we went through his assignments together. He told me that he wanted to be a writer.

Shortly after my twenty-first birthday, I finished my secretarial course and got a diploma in shorthand, typing and basic accounting. On my last day, Alfred gave me a statue which I still treasure. It's a roughly carved figure of an African man. The man has wire bracelets on his ankles and around one of his wrists. His ears are weighed down by heavy metal rings. His hair is crinkled and receding, exposing his bony skull. He has an old grey blanket draped around him and sits hunched on a low stool. A V-shaped stick held in his hand brushes against his cheek, making the man seem lost in thought. Alfred said the stick reminded him of a ritual where a child is passed from one elder to another through the fork of a sapling. He said it was the traditional way of welcoming a child into the world. Alfred told me that, in his culture, a child confers immortality on its parents by making them into ancestors.

The living and the dead talk to each other. Alfred said the ancestors are a white shadow, a legacy, that lives on in the world and also inside people; he said he called on his ancestral spirits when he needed help. He said his black shadow reminded him that he had power for doing good or evil in the world. In Africa, as a person grows older, he or she gets closer to the ancestors and their wisdom. I never told my parents about my friendship with Alfred because my father would have said I was 'a kaffir-lover'.

I was given a one-way ticket to Cape Town for my twenty-first birthday. I got a job in the student affairs department at UCT and Gordon helped me find a flat. Alfred and I exchanged letters for a few months but my love affair with Gordon soon became the focal point of my life.

I learned that Alfred survived the Rhodesian war and qualified as a teacher. The Athol Desmond Study Centre is still there, helping children who're unable to cope with mainstream education learn basic literacy and numeracy skills. Alfred is a member of the advisory board for the study centre. Zimbabwe has one of the highest literacy rates in Africa.

While I was living in Cape Town, Justine and Derek got married. Soon after their wedding in 1977 they emigrated to Toronto, where Derek's sister had been living for many years. My mother was distraught and her diary entries over the next few years evidenced the great sense of loss she felt after Justine moved away.

Fifteen

At the beginning of 1981, my parents announced they were coming to visit us. Gordon and I were living in Johannesburg at the time. My mother said they had an appointment at the Canadian Embassy in Pretoria for an interview concerning their application to emigrate to Toronto. This was the first I knew that there were plans afoot for them to go and live in Toronto with Justine and Derek.

During their visit, my mother told me she'd had an abortion in Pretoria during the war. I didn't think to ask her whose baby it was or where the abortion had taken place. I guess she was worried about me living with Gordon and not being married to him. It was still illegal to have an abortion in South Africa in the 1980's and just as scandalous to have a baby out of wedlock.

A few weeks later Lionel and Susan received confirmation they had been cleared for emigration to Canada, with a right of abode to live in Toronto. They left Zimbabwe on 24th August 1981 and never returned. They shared Justine and Derek's three-bedroomed apartment, which my mother called their 'Canadian kibbutz'.

Gordon and I had been married for eighteen months when the South African authorities created a tri-cameral parliament to represent whites, coloureds and Indians. I wrote to Elaine and told her I couldn't bear living there. She replied, offering us shelter for as long as we needed. So, on 14th February 1986 we went to stay with Elaine in Camden. Gordon got a transfer to the London office of his company and we bought a flat in North London. I got a job as a typesetter and joined the Anti-Apartheid Movement. I road my bike to the AAM offices to help with administrative jobs; I picketed outside South Africa House on Trafalgar Square. We joined a tennis club and settled into our new life in England.

In October 1987, my parents flew to London to celebrate Elaine's fortieth birthday; Yael and his wife flew over to be with us. That evening a hurricane decimated the southeast of England. Hampstead Heath looked as if a bomb had hit it. It would be the last time that Elaine, Yael and I were to sit around a table with our parents.

Blue Remembered Sky

PART THREE

Susan and Lionel

I believe that the real, dreadful quality of maternal tiredness is the mother's sense of struggling against prevailing disrespect. The baby may tire her, but we, if we aren't careful, can exhaust her.'

Naomi Stadlen

Two parents can't raise a child any more than one. You need a whole community – everybody – to raise a child. The notion that the head is the one who brings in the most money is a patriarchal notion, that a woman – and I have raised two children, alone – is somehow lesser than a male head. Or that I am incomplete without the male. It just doesn't work. It doesn't work for white people or black people. Why are we hanging onto it? I don't know. It isolates people into little units – people need a larger unit.

Toni Morrison

We understand that the prohibition against men expressing any emotion other than anger has ramifications for world and domestic peace. We all know what the world tells girls they cannot do and boys what they cannot feel. Like feminist parents every-where, lesbian parents strive to encourage our sons to embrace all kinds of emotions. We encourage them to develop nonviolent methods of negotiation. We teach our sons self-sufficiency in terms of domestic chores like cooking, sewing and picking up after themselves … and it is not just to avoid the domestic servitude of another generation of women; self-sufficiency is, in itself, a tremendous gift.

Jess Wells

Blue Remembered Sky

Part Three

One

Sandi takes her time looking through the documents that I've brought along. The pieces of paper she's sifting through hold clues about my past. They are part of the memorabilia that Justine sent me after clearing out our parents' apartment. I've had so little sleep recently that my head feels as foggy as the weather outside.

"I feel like I'm drowning." I try not to cry. I'd driven over to Sandi's house before the rush hour. Being able to concentrate, let alone having to deal with icy conditions and heavy traffic just compounds my worry. Sandi looks at me and nods. She's moved the furniture around so that her chair is facing the window. I've spent months gazing past her shoulder at the pattern of birds on her white curtains. Now I have to look more directly at her face.

"When you speak to me, it's like you're under water with me." Tears start rolling down my cheeks. Sandi smiles at me in her gentle way and I take a handful of tissues out of the box on the table next to me. We sit together quietly until my tears subside.

"Yael ... Yael found their marriage certificate after they'd sold our house. It was when they were living at Esperanza; Yael was looking through the drawers in my mother's dressing table for a cigarette. It was a real shock when he told me because my mother never mentioned that she'd been married to Benjamin Steinberg. I still don't know much about it except that one of his daughters is a beautiful actress who made her name in a James Bond movie with Roger Moore. I used to dream of contacting her to see if she could tell me anything ... but she'd have thought I was just another deranged fortune hunter ..."

Sandi looks carefully at other bits and pieces of paper, my father's graduation certificate from medical school and the various registration documents he needed to practise.

She sits back, hugging her red cardigan around her, and pulling her pleated skirt more snugly around her knees. I open my bag and hand her a crinkled piece of paper.

"Here's my father's birth certificate. Can you see where he's crossed out his name? His handwriting was so messy ..." *I watch Sandi carefully as she studies it.*

"Can you see that my grandfather's occupation is different to the one on their marriage certificate?" *Sandi puts the two pieces of paper next to each other.*

"Ah, yes, I can see that," *Sandi says, looking from one document to the other.*

"It's obvious the one on their marriage certificate wasn't true. My father lied about so many things ..." *I drop my soggy tissue in the bin next to the couch. I can feel the sting of a rush of desperation. My thoughts swim against a tidal surge. The tremors that make me hold onto the wall next to my bed at night force me to dig my hands into my lap. For a second or two, it feels like I'm going to lose consciousness; I have to make a concentrated effort to bring my attention back.*

"There are so many things that don't make sense ... all these terrible dreams that wake me up, this shaking ..." *Tears well up again.* "And ... and getting an email from Penny all these years later ... finding out all this other stuff ..."

My chest feels so tight I can hardly breathe. Sandi sits quietly.

She leans forward. Very gently she says, "It's best we do this work in manageable chunks, Charlie."

Part Three

Two

Between 1990 and 1995, I corresponded with my parents in an effort to gain a deeper understanding of them, whilst also trying to make sense of my childhood. In one of her first letters, my mother wrote: *"Why did you run away and hide when we lived at Ingutsheni? Was it because you were too scared to face an angry parent? Or was it to punish (presumably) me for accusing you? I've never understood the motive for your running off over several years. You asked me, in a letter, about why I was frightened when you ran away. Well, it was partly because of the environment: seven hundred acres of bush and some of the inhabitants were known to be crazy in one way or another. Also, there were hazards in the animal and reptile species at Ingutsheni and there was the quarry as well, sometimes filled with water. All these hazards were fact but also, I didn't understand what made you take off – if you were angry, frightened, what went on inside your head? Lots of children run off but most announce their intention. I used to do it as a child myself, which gave my mother time to pack a tiny attaché case, take me by the hand and push me and the case out of the front door, say "good-bye" and shut the door firmly on me. This was such a shock to me that I set off defiantly, but by the time I reached the gate to the lane we lived on, I was too attached to my home to go further. But you didn't do that – you just vanished."*

I never went very far in the beginning. It was easy for me to disappear into the tall grass just beyond the periphery of the garden. I stayed there for hours and was soon engrossed in the comings and goings of the world around me. I would feast my eyes on iridescent sunbirds, swallowtail butterflies, blue-winged wasps and guinea fowl would cackle to each other. I eventually made my way home when I felt hungry. As I got older, when something upset or frightened me, I would shout "You'll miss me when I'm gone" as I retreated into my bedroom, slamming the door behind me. My mother's letter awoke something inside me; a fragment, a reminder of an intangible, daily dread that I couldn't name.

In March 1992, Justine phoned to say my mother was seriously ill and was not expected to live. I flew to Toronto expecting the worst. Elaine arrived the next day and we took turns at visiting my mother in the hospital. She had changed from the robust and energetic woman I had known to an emaciated person in a hospital bed and it shocked me deeply. She was painfully frail and woefully short of breath due to the emphysema that was clogging up her lungs. She was clearly unhappy about her lack of privacy and her bed looked so cold and clinical that it broke my heart. I got a teddy bear to keep her company. I bought her a copy of The Velveteen Rabbit because I wanted her to know how much I loved her in case she just stopped breathing and passed away. It was an agonising time. I stayed for five weeks and she got visibly stronger during the time I was there. Not long after I flew back to England, my mother refused to stay in hospital any longer and was discharged into Lionel's care with a portable oxygen machine.

My mother was generous in her memories and the letters she wrote me conveyed a strong sense of her early life and her background. Her parents, Alice May Comins and Percival Thomas Smith were married on 10th January 1916 in the Parish Church at Matson in Gloucestershire. Susan was born exactly nine months later on 29th October. She was their only child.

Letter dated 24th November 1990: *"When I was a small girl, I used to walk with my Grandma every Sunday to put fresh flowers on the graves of my uncle and grandpa. I still remember the awful smell of the old water in the vase, as I emptied it and refilled it for the new offering! I can remember too thinking this was a silly thing to do, because two men would not appreciate flowers in such a smelly container. But I could only do as I was told, so very unwillingly I brought the vase, now filled with cold water, back to my Grandma, who put her flowers in and plonked the vase back in the grave until the next Sunday – and our visit! The grave was for my father's family only – my mother was cremated and it is just as well, she would have hated to be buried, especially with Emma Smith, her mother-in-law, with whom she had nothing in common; there was no love lost between those two strong personalities."*

Letter dated 30th October 1990: *"My mother was Irish in every typical way. Black hair, blue eyes, wonderful complexion, a great vitality and a free spirit. She was never a lover of domesticity and longed to travel, which she did from very soon after my father's death, until her own some twenty years later.*

Percival Thomas Smith (my father) was English, born in Gloucester. He had a brother who died young of TB, which was rife in those days. His father William died of it too. My mother was as extravert as my father was introvert. He was a loving man, who sang songs when he was happy – to me – and read a lot, was interested in politics, wood working in his shed in the garden, made wonderful jams, marmalade, pickles, etc., smoked a pipe, had silver hair from age thirty. I only realized what a darling man I had for a father when I decided to become a nurse. He was so supportive of this career for me and helped to withstand my mother's violent opposition, to stay with it and to prove to myself that I was capable of seeing it through to the end and giving him that satisfaction, which was all he ever asked of me. He, like me, loved dogs and always had a devoted spaniel. He didn't earn much, but he was much loved by the men who worked with him and they respected him as I do – still."

I went to visit the family grave in Matson, Gloucestershire. It was easy to find the big headstone bearing the names of my great-grandparents Emma and William Smith, as well as their son William, my grandfather Percival's brother. My grandfather Percy died long before I was born, so I didn't know him at all. I wondered where he was buried because his name wasn't on the Smith family headstone. I saw that William died on 2nd May 1903, aged twenty-four. He was nine years older than Percy, who was born in 1888. My great-grandfather William died on 28th February 1909, aged fifty-two, and my great-grandmother Emma on 29th December 1934 aged eighty. I imagined my mother having to trail along with her mother, Percy and Emma to visit the graves of her grandfather and uncle, just as she described in her letter. The church, St Katherine's, was over the road from a stately home called Matson House. I stood and looked at the grand house over the way and I wondered whether Emma had worked there as a domestic servant. My great-grandfather William Smith had worked as a porter at Gloucester railway station, as had my great-uncle William. The Smith's were clearly a working-class family.

Letter dated 29th November 1990: *"Senior was Basingstoke High School (for girls) as opposed to the Grammar School (for boys). The house in Basingstoke was 7 Penrith Road and I walked to school with my black dog Sam. 'Crossway' was very different when Lionel and I lived there. The houses on either side were not there. The land was my father's. We had a field to live in, with Crossway squarely in the middle and the whole area was farmland where we walked and gathered holly for*

Christmas and mushrooms in September/October. My mother loved living there and had many animals – rabbits, goats, dogs, chickens, cats – one rabbit was a pet and hopped up the stairs and into bed with her! My mother was very interfering!! It never stopped and Lionel really resented her on that score. He was always right in his opinion, so who was this old woman? It made my life, up until her death, very difficult and conflicted but you were all such a source of happiness to me, that I don't remember being especially bothered by her. Although she thought I was far too soft a mother and not 'in control' of you all!! No discipline!"

Before my mother went to train as a nurse, she worked as an au pair in Germany and had a brief romance. Like many young people at that time, her boyfriend belonged to the Hitler youth.

Letter dated 24th November 1990: *"I've enclosed a photograph of the German family with whom I lived from 1935 - December 1936. Started at University College Hospital January 4th 1937, a date I will never forget - my entry into the real world! My father died in, I think, 1943. I was in Durban and mail was very difficult to receive, but I know he was fifty-six years old and I think he would have been buried in the family plot at Matson, a village near Gloucester."*

It's unclear what happened to Crossway and where my grandparents were living by the time my mother left home in 1935, the year after her paternal grandmother Emma Smith died. There was no sign of Percival Thomas at the family grave in Matson. I assume that Alice had his body cremated and his ashes scattered or perhaps interred in the churchyard at Old Basing where they'd lived. I wondered whether my mother's training at University College Hospital had other attractions like free accommodation and a city like London to enjoy after her rural upbringing. How else did an only child get away from her parents in 1937 without being married?

Her next letter suggests there were issues with money at home. It's hard now to imagine how few opportunities there were in the 1930's and 1940's for women, until the war changed a lot of things. Universities were still bastions of male privilege and the BBC discriminated against divorcees until after the Second World War.

Letter dated 14th March 1991: *"I, not Lionel have a regard for money in terms of power and honesty. I grew up being used by my mother as a messenger to debt collectors. She always sent ME to pay a bit off an account here, an account there and I always felt ashamed. She also did a very bad thing to my father – she used me to take money from his account. He'd sold his mother's house on her death and deposited an amount in his account. I still don't know for sure but I suspect she forged his signature and I was sent to collect the amounts she took. I was very young, maybe sixteen years old but I knew enough to know this was wrong, because she always warned me not to tell. I was too frightened of her to disobey but vowed in myself that I would never do that to my husband if I ever married. Then later, I marry Lionel, who truly has no idea of how to manage money but has implicit faith in my ability to manage our affairs."*

Alice Comins came from a middle-class family. My great-grandfather, Robert Comins, was an engineer. Alice and Percy lived at 'Crossway' where my mother spent much of her childhood. I wonder if Percy and his working-class background didn't quite live up to the lifestyle my Granny Alice was accustomed to? On their marriage certificate, Percy's occupation is listed as 'fitter and turner on the railways'. I speculated that perhaps Alice had developed a habit of living beyond their means and was often in debt. Towards the end of her life, she worked as a governess for an opera singer, and travelled with her to the

United States, where she died of a stroke. I think the most likely explanation for my grandmother's devious financial dealings was that the proceeds of selling Crossway, my grandmother's family home, were deposited in her husband Percy's account, and the only way she could access the money was through subterfuge. Women often didn't have personal bank accounts in those days. My mother Susan never had her own bank account.

Letter dated 19 November 1992: *"I was christened on Christmas Day 1916 in Old Basing Church. Confirmed in the Church of England in the Cathedral at Winchester by the Bishop, sometime in the summer of 1934. Ben Steinberg and I married on 10th December 1940 in St. Pancras Registry Office, with all parents present as well as my friends Barbara and Elizabeth. Lionel and I married in Camberwell Registry Office on Saturday January 25th, 1947."*

Letter dated 27th January 1991: *"Lionel and I celebrated forty-four years of marriage on Friday. How we've survived each other, I don't know! But we're still able to discuss our respective opinions and more calmly than in the early years, when we were so convinced that the view that each held was the only correct one. Now we know that each is entitled to a view and they don't have to coincide. We do care very much for each other's well-being and treat each other with respect and concern. In fact, we still love each other. You ask how we met – at work. I was the sister of the 'staff ward', he came one day to talk with a sick sister on my ward, and there it was, love hit us, and we did not do anything apart from then on. I had left Ben approximately eighteen months and Lionel was just back from Abyssinia, as it was where he had been with an Air Force squadron as their Medical Officer. Neither of us had any reservations. We just were young, and he was ready to have a wife. Unfortunately, I was not free to be his wife then, but we waited until World War*

Two ended and then we went to England. Ben divorced me and Lionel and I married in London on January 25th, 1947. You remember the 'Annual General' party we used to have? That was always near the 25th January and we celebrated our marriage at that party each year. It became a fixture in all our lives – the friends too!"

My mother often talked about the wounded airmen she nursed in the Burns Unit at University College Hospital after the outbreak of war. She said the men were known as 'guinea pigs' for the new skin grafting techniques that were used to help them recover from horrific burns. She said they were the bravest men in the world. There's a picture of her in her nurse's uniform at the Springfield Military Hospital. The handwriting on the back of the frame tells me it was taken in 1942. When I look at that photo, I wonder who my mother was in love with – her husband Ben, or my father.

In 2015, twenty-five years after Ben Steinberg's death, I was able to obtain a copy of his war record. I discovered he had been posted to South Africa eight days after he and my mother were married. Ben left for a posting in Belgium on 4th June 1944, leaving my mother behind in South Africa. The time they'd spent in Durban was a lot longer than I had previously thought. Did Susan dread going to Europe with the war raging and bombs falling? Had she met my father and fallen out of love with her husband? Did Ben ask for a posting elsewhere because he discovered his wife was having an affair? My mother told Justine that Ben was too close to his mother for her liking. No matter how many times Yael or I asked her about her first marriage, she always replied that it was a wartime marriage and a rush of blood to the head.

Letter dated 8th December 1990: *"Thank you for sending me Ben's obituary. Barbara sent me one too. Ben was such a dynamic person, inventive, witty and kind but, sadly, terribly moody and that's why I wouldn't live with him. I'd* *grown up with constant drama – with my mother – and longed to live a gentle, quiet country life. Take care, dear child, and be happy."*

Ben's obituary was in two mainstream English newspapers when he died: *"Benjamin Steinberg was born of Jewish parents of East European origin in the East End of London. His father was a barber, his mother a waitress and then a buttonhole-maker in the rag-trade and together they eventually built up a wholesale business. Ben won a scholarship to Highbury County School and University College Hospital, from which he went soon after qualifying, first as a civilian Medical Officer in the Royal Air Force Voluntary Reserve, and then after the outbreak of the Second World War, as a serving officer. He was based in South Africa, Belgium (where he was responsible for the early use of penicillin against sexually transmitted diseases, both in the Services and in the civilian population) and finally in Germany. He was twice mentioned in despatches and achieved the rank of Squadron leader. After the war he returned to London and his major interest, obstetrics. He was consultant to four London hospitals and became Fellow of the Royal College of Obstetricians and Gynaecologists in 1965. Together with Steptoe and Edwards, he founded the British Fertility Society. He was a popular teacher of midwives and junior doctors. He had enormous vitality and would often work a full two sessions at the hospital, see other patients at home or in a clinic and then go to the theatre, opera or ballet."*

One day during a visit to London, my mother showed me where she had slept in the Underground station at Embankment during the Blitz. I remember thinking how terrifying that period of her life must have been and how much she'd probably enjoyed fleeing the devastation in London when Ben was posted to South Africa in 1941.

I wonder when my mother discovered she was pregnant. She told me she had stayed in a Catholic Nursing Home called Nazareth House in Pretoria. It was a home for unmarried mothers and it was run by a Mrs Maynard. My mother always spoke fondly of this lady, with whom she had kept in touch after the war. In her battered old address-book, I saw Mrs Maynard passed away in 1977 and my mother had written 'R.I.P.' where she'd crossed out her name.

I don't know whether the baby she was carrying was my father's, but I assume that it was. I didn't think to ask when she told me she'd had an abortion because her words came out of the blue and took me by surprise.

Letter dated 1st March 1991: *"You ask about how I felt about having an abortion. I still, to this day, feel sad when I think of it. However, there was no choice. I did not want a child at that time – my life was a mess. I had to leave the army nursing service before "my condition" became obvious, so I followed Lionel to Pretoria and found a doctor in Joburg who was willing and able to perform abortions. So off I went, and it was done. I didn't feel guilty – just sad to say good-bye to this little victim of circumstance and I still wonder what he (it was a male) would have become, had he been allowed to live?"*

Abortion was illegal at the time my mother was faced with this painful decision. The fact that she had to wait until she was four months pregnant meant her baby was well formed. It's likely the baby was dismembered during the procedure. This must have been a deeply traumatic experience.

I think that the earlier an abortion is carried out the better. I would support my daughter and my son whatever decision they made in such circumstances. I'm thankful I've not had to make that choice myself. I've often thought how painful it must have been for my mother to remember losing that baby boy as we, her surviving children, all blossomed and grew up. I wish she'd been able to talk about it with me as I grew up. I think she was very brave to have lived with her secret so discreetly hidden away, and I'm proud that I am the one she chose to tell.

I got a copy of my grandfather Percy's death certificate and found that, on 27th June 1943, he died of bowel cancer.

I thought again about Ben being posted to Belgium in 1944 and my mother staying behind in South Africa. I considered her getting the news of her father's death and her reluctance to go back to the battlefront in Europe, so I'm not surprised she fell into my father's arms. Though I will never know exactly why or when she did.

Three

When I looked through her letters and diaries, I found that my mother had kept in touch with her housemaid Martha after they emigrated to Canada. I found this odd, considering she had accused Martha of stealing from her and often mimicked the way she spoke English. I guess the relationship between madam and servant was a complex one, given that so many African women helped European women run their immaculate homes and raise their immaculate children. My father called Martha a 'stupid black cow' when she dropped the sizzling roasting dish on the table when it burned her hand. Nobody took Martha to hospital to receive medical attention and money was taken off her wages to repair the table. I feel ashamed to recall that when my mother bought our servants their food rations, she gave them the same offcuts as the meat she fed to her bulldogs. My parents made Martha redundant when they emigrated to Canada.

Letter dated 21st February 1991: *"Lionel had such agony of mind trying to accept a 'black' government. He is very obsessive and was at that time, totally obsessed with fear and hate towards Dr Ushiwokunze, the then Minister of Health. He has, of course, by now forgotten all of that – and the fact that he told me over and over, that we would not be able to travel anywhere now that the 'blacks' had taken over."*

Her letter titled 'Thanks-Giving Day' is about a journey to visit Justine and Derek's friends.

Letter dated 8th October 1990: *"The Lows are in the process of building their house and it stands in 'The Matopos' of the Ontario Lake District! There are huge boulders and lichens surrounding Sugar Lake on whose shores the house (not nearly completed) is situated. It was a dull grey and the colours of the surrounding forests looked really stunning. But it was cold - that awful cold that makes one shake. I was the most warmly dressed of all. Pam had thin cotton pants, Ross had a T shirt, as did Justine. Derek wore shorts, no socks and a T shirt. We looked a miserable bunch. We lurched and stumbled into their house, slipping and sliding, Justine holding my hand which, for some reason, made me totally stupid. Somehow, we all made it to the half-finished house. They have really wrought a miracle, these two, working only on weekends. The resemblance to the Matopos is uncanny and during the time we were there, freezing and eating non-stop, we saw the rain sweep across in a great, grey curtain over the surface of the lake. Ross explained to me that in a few* *weeks' time they will be able to ski down from the house onto the lake, by then, frozen and have fun cross-country skiing – can you imagine? After we had eaten everything we had brought, with sighs of relief, we set off home. The drive back was fairly uneventful. We drove in and out of rain squalls and the car warmed us up. Then we came to that horrid place on the road – an accident, not on our side of the road. A young boy was waving traffic on and a body covered by a red blanket lay in the road between two partially destroyed cars. People stood around – no police or ambulance yet. It was a disturbing scene. However, we continued on and soon came home. Derek drove straight to our house. I asked them in for a drink to warm them up, but they declined, and I was glad for that. I was still shaken by the accident. Lionel and I went in and switched off the air conditioner. I made Lionel a good stiff whisky, me a sherry and later we had a bowl of soup, then went to bed to read.*

I dreamt of the crash as if I was floating above it, trying to get down and ask them how did they have a red blanket? In my nursing life a red blanket was a signal of an emergency, so how did those unfortunate people have a red blanket to wrap that body in? It still bothers me – it was probably just a co-incidence but odd. So that was my Thanks-Giving Sunday.

If you are still reading by now (I'll not keep you much longer) we have just had an election in Ontario, and to my delight, the N.D.P. have won for the first time!! So, we have what most Canadians think of as a 'Communist' Government. In fact, it's just Socialist and I'm pleased to say there are eleven women in the Cabinet and thirteen men. They have only been in for a week, so can't comment on performance yet.

Anyway, my dear Charlotte, thank you for being the caring daughter you are. You know how much I love you and always will. Susan. P.S. Be Happy!"

Her dream about floating over the crash made me think about accidents of birth, accidents of love and accidents of war.

Letter dated 2nd April 1991: *"You ask me what used to frustrate me when you were all small children? In a word – Lionel. He was too busy being the good doctor, to be concerned about my role as the mother of a family. He, as I've told you before trusted me to "know the answers" and if I didn't, then I wasn't a "good mother" and should "grow up" myself, and that didn't do much for me! He always felt that we were under his control or I felt that, and whilst I resented this feeling, I had a need to please him. So, I accepted criticism even though I felt I didn't deserve it and I was angry and resentful of it. All that stupidity of making everything tidy before he came home in the evening made me frustrated. I so wanted him to be a part of the daily life of us all but he remained aloof and critical. So, when he went to Salisbury every month for two days, I felt like a bird flying free; we had picnics and sat outside in the dark looking at stars and eating food which Lionel didn't enjoy and we all did. Later in your lives, I used to take us out for lunch when he was at his Rotary meetings just to have that sense of choice and freedom. Individually, I didn't know what to do when Justine was a baby and didn't sleep. My instinct was to take her into our room and into my bed until she slept and put her back in her cot. However, Lionel didn't approve and told me I was spoiling her. I was too tired to care and did that any way until it dawned on me that she was just 'lonely'. So, I moved her cot in with us and she slept all night very quickly! It was wonderful!!*

Elaine was a cause of dissention between us too. Lionel was very strict about punctuality and she used to forget to come in for lunch on time when she was at Junior School. She had friends around the neighbourhood and came in late (in the holidays) to lunch. It upset me to see her punished so harshly but I had to appear to agree so that Lionel and I presented a 'united front'. I agree with punctuality; I think it's an attribute that should be emphasised in one's dealings with children. I just didn't approve of the punishment for forgetfulness at age seven - it seemed excessive.

You used to upset me very much by running away but you know that. You also used to upset me when you were older by asking me to help you with homework, and then crying because you couldn't remember dates! It seemed to me such an emotional response to something which really only required 'parrot' learning. You were probably crying for another reason – one which I didn't guess at – otherwise I might have been less impatient with you.

Poor children you all suffered but so did I, and so did Lionel. But I can still be angry that he claims to be so proud of you, individually and collectively, when it seems to me that none of us ever managed, long ago, to do anything to please or earn praise from him. I think I've learned a lot about 'acceptance' in my life; that one cannot expect another person to change unless that person truly sees a reason to change, and only then will the change happen. In the meantime, love must be unconditional and constant."

Letter dated 9th April 1991: *"I was impatient sometimes but that was because I felt that you, nor the others, paid attention to me. Lionel was effective in enforcing discipline and I was not and that made me feel ineffectual. Lionel says he hoped very much that you, being such a bright child would follow his steps and graduate from the University of Cape Town. I hope this explains his behaviour when you walked away from an academic career. I thought you would enjoy being at university, playing 1st team tennis, having friends with you, although I hated the idea of sending children to be 'educated' in South Africa when there was a good multi-racial* *university in Rhodesia. My political thinking was not popular with anyone."*

Letter dated 24th November 1990: *"One should be able to achieve. I thought this would help your confidence in your abilities and you would be glad you had more to offer than just clever tricks with make-up. It's such a pity that children are either not able to express their feelings verbally – or if they can – they are ignored by their parents, who, for all they love their children, can't bear to be told that they are on the 'wrong road', and so don't listen. However, the mitigating factor is that parents, although they make mistakes, are usually acting out of a passionate love for the child, so they should be forgiven."*

I remember that her final letter upset me very deeply. I wished that I'd been able to turn the clock back and change my relationship with her. It's clear in all her letters that she loved me and did her best at a time when women's voices were not heard. I think that she found it cathartic to write to me, to tell me about her feelings for my father and the major events in her life.

Four

It was a bitterly cold the day when I went to the Sunnybrook hospital to say goodbye to my mother. She was rallying well and wanted to go home. After I left her bedside, I went to a nearby playground and sat on a swing in the icy sunshine. I swung myself as high as I could. I didn't cry because I just wanted to get back to England to resume my life as far away from my parents as possible. She died eight months later, on 21st February 1993.

Part Three

I waited for Justine to summon me to Toronto for Susan's funeral, but nothing happened. Susan had made it clear she didn't want any fuss after her death. There was to be no funeral and no memorial service. I asked Justine to post my mother's ashes to me. A few weeks later, the postman brought them as a special delivery to my door. I put them in the cupboard under the stairs and forgot about them.

Emily was born later that year. I remember pushing my beautiful baby along in her pram feeling utterly elated that I was raising a child in such an ordinary way. When my baby was ten days old, I decided to scatter my mother's ashes in the River Thames. It was a cold October day, but the sun shone brightly as we walked down to the river. Gordon wore the baby inside his coat, and I pushed the box of ashes along in the baby buggy. I took the plastic bag out of its black box and chose a spot I would remember. As I leaned over the water's edge, a curious swan sailed over, thinking I was scattering some bits of bread for it to eat. Gordon and I walked along the tow path once the ceremony was over. I was looking at the iridescent blue and green feathers on a mallard duck squatting nearby when the word 'suicide' flashed into my mind. I wondered why on earth such a thought had popped into my head. As we walked back home, I thought about my father living on his own in Toronto but most of all I wished my mother had lived to see my new baby.

Something about the timing of her death made me feel uncomfortable. I wondered if my decision not to visit again had disappointed her and dented her will to live. Eventually I asked Justine what she thought - if she thought my mother had committed suicide. Justine said Susan had put everything in order before she died. There were only a few precious pieces of jewellery and a minimum of clothes left behind. When I asked Elaine and Yael for their thoughts, we discovered my mother had phoned each of us in turn on the day she died. I was the last one on her list. It was a Sunday afternoon, not long after lunch, when she phoned. I was a few weeks' pregnant and I remember we spent quite a bit of time discussing names for the baby. During our conversation she warned me that there was a dark side to pregnancy. I dismissed her comment and put the phone down soon after feeling slightly irritated with her.

Justine and I have come to accept my mother reached a point where her ill health had become intolerable and she decided the time had come to end her life.

Justine wrote: *"You say the shock of Mum's dying made your memory shut down. For me it seems the shock made it stay forever. I had come back from doing a show in Edmonton on the Thursday mid-afternoon and began setting up the one in Toronto immediately. Later that night I went to say hello to Lionel and Susan, and we decided that, since the show would be occupying all my time Friday, Saturday, etc., we agreed that on Wednesday night I'd go shopping. I said I'd pop in on Friday and drop off whatever we were going to have for a nice dinner on the Tuesday night, as it was on my way home. I said Derek would meet us there. I bought veal and some yellow freesias as the weather was gloomy.*

On the Sunday at the gift show, it was extremely busy with a huge snowstorm outside and I was a bit ticked because everyone was going to the Boswell's for their son's engagement party, which was at two in the afternoon and there I was working again. As you know Susan was really weak, having to have oxygen all the time; she was very thin, but she was quite happy and I thought, looking forward to veal in white wine sauce for dinner on Tuesday.

In those days we didn't have cell phones but fortunately the company always rented a phone for the shows otherwise it meant no one could contact any of us all day. So, when it rang around two o'clock someone else answered it and called Chris, who then came and quietly told me I should go to Sunnybrook as my Mum had died. At first, I thought it was one of Derek's jokes. Then I phoned him at the Green's, and he said Lionel had phoned

Debbie because he couldn't reach either of us. Lionel told Debbie he'd already called 911, so presumably he went in the ambulance to Sunnybrook because that's where I eventually found him in his brown jacket, after sitting in the snow on the Don Valley.

When I got there, I just left my car on the street in the snow because finding a space would have taken too long and I thought she might still be alive, so was racing around to find out where she was. When I did, they asked me to go and identify her.

She had her green dress, long strand of pearls and her ivory earrings, looking perfectly peaceful. I've always wondered if she had saved enough pills to send her off peacefully, having talked to Elaine and Yael in the morning and then you in the afternoon. We'll never know."

Five

When I was in my teens, I asked my father what made him want to be a psychiatrist. He told me that he'd done an experiment to do with the placebo effect during his training at the Maudsley Hospital. He said it had sparked an interest for him in the power of the mind.

When I was thirty-five and he was seventy-nine, I wrote to him for the first time in my life and asked him to tell me about his childhood.

Letter dated 19th July 1990: *"I have never regretted taking up Medicine and later Psychiatry. I enjoy people and found endless pleasure in helping people and also getting to know about people. I think, although I say it myself, that I was a good psychiatrist who would listen and was also well liked. My only medical problem while in Rhodesia was my colleague Dr. Hamilton who took* *advantage of a few months' seniority to me in the Rhodesian Mental Health Service and tended to make life rather difficult.*

I think I was a good father to you and the others and was always very conscious of my need to give as much time as my work allowed to you. I have always had a great regard and respect for Susan's opinion and because of this, encouraged her to take much more part in all your lives than perhaps other fathers did.

I was born in Cape Town as you know, the only boy in a family of three sisters who in retrospect, I think rather resented me and the fact that I was the only one who went to University. I do know that after both my parents died, not long after I qualified and was doing my first house job in Maritzburg, they tended to sponge on me in a manner I could ill afford. So, I cannot say my relationship with them became very happy and I was relieved to be able to live away from them.

My biggest weakness was my disinterest in money, and I think I might have been a much wealthier man than I am today. Though I have no regrets in this regard and never fail to be impressed with the way Susan manages our finances and how well we live. My biggest fright was the heart attack I had after we had settled down to live in Canada. It was awful and certainly put me off cigarettes permanently. My recollections of it cause me concern that Justine, as well as Yael, continue to smoke but it is not for me to try to interfere with their habits, even if I could.

I think you are a very lucky girl to have Gordon as a husband. He always has treated me with respect which I appreciate, and he gives me a sense of security, as far as his ability to maintain you and look after you. I want to wish you a very happy birthday and to thank you and Gordon for the financial assistance you give Susan and I now we are living on our own, which is a very great improvement to sharing Justine's apartment. I have found many of the tenants here of the same mind, many of them having lived with one or other of their children and then finding the independence of life away from them a great relief. I am very satisfied with the way all of you have turned out and it gives Susan and I great joy when we hear of Derek's children, as well as his sister's children. Also we see the fate of so many young people here in Toronto. Again, my dear daughter, I enjoyed writing to you and please give all my love and regards to your excellent husband – Lionel."

I remember reading my father's letter and saying to Gordon that his attitude towards me made me feel more like a motor car than a human being.

When I was living in Cape Town, a plump woman with dark hair called by at my flat. She said she was my cousin Desiree. I must have looked at her blankly when she told me her mother's name because I had no idea who she was talking about. I don't remember how long she stayed, or even whether I invited her in for a cup of tea. If I told my parents about her visit nobody made an effort to explain how Desiree came to be my cousin. That fleeting moment is all I recall, because my father never talked about his family.

Justine reminded me about an occasion when our Aunt Karin called by at our house in Suburbs. She was visiting her son Alex who lived in Khumalo, a largely Jewish suburb nearby. Justine remembered my mother coming to the door and telling Karin my father was ill with the flu and wouldn't be able to get out of bed. Justine laughed and asked me if I remembered Alex's two daughters, who were at Townsend High School when we were there. She said it was unbelievable that, when my father left Ingutsheni and started his private practice, he and his cousin Alex had worked in the same building. Justine said, as far as she knew, they never spoke to each other. My father mentioned Alex Abelman in one of his letters: *"There always was a great deal of friction between Alex and myself and for that matter, between him and the medical profession. Although one does not like speaking ill of the dead, Alex unfortunately was very money minded and as a practising gynaecologist tended to encourage his patients to have hysterectomies and for that matter abortions, regrettably not always on a sound medical basis."*

In 1990, in an effort to find out more about my father, I contacted the South African Broadcasting Corporation and put out an appeal for lost relatives. I remember the excitement I felt when I got a call from a man named Brian who turned out to be my first cousin. Brian is the son of my Aunt Ethel, the youngest child in my father's family. He told me my grandmother's name for the first time – Ruby. I asked if my grandfather's name was Mordechai and whether it was true that he had been a rabbi. Brian laughed and said he wouldn't have called Mordechai a rabbi, more like a devout man who went to the synagogue often. He went on to tell me about my father's other two sisters, Karin the eldest and Ruth, the second child in the family. Ruth was in a nursing home and Karin was no longer alive. So, my father was the third child in his family - like me.

My excitement grew when, a few weeks later, I received a letter from Brian's mother, my Aunt Ethel. She was delighted to have found me, having not heard from my father for over forty years. She begged me for my father's address in Toronto. I wrote back, my letter brimming with curiosity about the past. I asked her to send me some photographs of my father and his family because I'd never met any of them. I sent her my father's contact details and waited in anticipation for her reply.

Her second letter was utterly different in tone. She told me it was futile to re-open old wounds and it was best to leave matters as they were. There were no photographs and I never heard from her again. My father thanked me for putting him back in touch with his sister but I'm not sure if he ever did reply to Ethel's letter. Maybe she'd sent him her phone number, hoping he'd ring her up, and that's why her second letter to me was so cold.

I bombarded him with questions. He wrote back in his illegible writing on self-sealing aerogram letters. I pored over his scrawl in disbelief and my sense of frustration grew at how little he was prepared to share of himself:

Letter dated 29th October 1990: *"Of course, as a healthy young man I had many girlfriends, particularly when I was a young house surgeon at Greys Hospital in Pietermaritzburg, and I sported a pair of tails and white waistcoat when we went dancing most Saturday nights. Justine was indeed one of my cherished girlfriends and you are quite right that in my romantic way, I suggested the name for Justine to which Susan had no objection. All my love to Gordon and to you."*

I tried to find more relatives and Brian put me in touch with Shelley, my Aunt Karin's granddaughter. Shelley was thrilled to be in touch, and we exchanged many letters. She helped me understand much about my father's background but still there were no photographs.

Shelley wrote: *"Once upon a time Leib Perelman was born in Vienna, Austria. Leib married and had two children, Ezra and Mordechai. Leib was born to a very wealthy family. He himself was a banker. It was his desire to go to Jerusalem to die. (This is the desire of every Jew and every year we traditionally say to one another "next year in Jerusalem"). He arrived in Jerusalem and settled in Mao Shoarim. This is a very, very religious part of Jerusalem. The people who live here are called 'Chassidic Jews'. They wear black dress and men have distinctive sideburns. Women wear head coverings, etc, etc. Mordechai married Ruby Silverman and the first of four children was born – Karin Perelman (1902).*

Now suddenly came the end of the Ottoman Empire in Palestine (i.e. Turkish rule). The Perelman family lost all their money. Both Ezra and Mordechai decided to emigrate to South Africa. Mordechai decided to emigrate to Cape Town in 1906 with his wife Ruby and daughter Karin (then 3 years old). His brother Ezra settled in Johannesburg where he worked as a brush maker. There is/was a branch of the Perelman family in Johannesburg.

Mordechai and Ruby settled in Cape Town. Mordechai died on 19th December 1937 of a coronary thrombosis at the age of sixty-four. Mordechai also worked as a brush maker. As I have already said, he was a respected member of the community and did a lot of work for the synagogue. The family were members of the Woodstock Synagogue. This was a respected end of town in those days. He gave his wife Ruby a hard time. I am not sure, but I seem to remember hearing that her health was not good. Ruby died of diabetes mellitus and a coronary thrombosis on 17th February 1937 aged fifty-seven.

Mordechai and Ruby's four children were: Karin – 1902-1981; Ruth – 1909; Leib – 5th November 1911 and Ethel – 1920."

Justine said that Desiree, the woman who'd knocked on the door of my flat in Plumstead was my Aunt Ruth's daughter. During the course of researching my father's family history, I discovered that Ezra disembarked from a freight ship in Cape Town in 1905. His age was listed as thirty-nine. Mordechai was sixty-four in 1937 when he died, so I worked out that Ezra was seven years older than his brother. My grandfather Mordechai had followed his brother Ezra to South Africa in 1906 with his young family. Ezra settled in Johannesburg. Mordechai set up home in a working-class area of Cape Town known as Salt River. A few blocks away from the family home, in the same street, he ran a hardware store.

Part Three

On his birth certificate Lionel crossed out his Hebrew name, Leib, and named himself 'Lionel'. On it, his father Mordechai's occupation is listed as 'draper' and his address is given as 'Albert Street, Salt River, Cape Town'. On my parent's Marriage Certificate in 1947, my grandfather Mordechai's occupation is listed as 'estate agent'. Mordechai's occupation on his own death certificate is listed as a 'general dealer'. Clearly my father fabricated a thing or two about his background when he married an attractive English nurse named Susan Steinberg in 1947. Perhaps, in the early days of their love affair, he'd assumed she was Jewish. Perhaps Susan had kept her marriage to Ben a secret until she discovered she was pregnant and they were then forced to face some difficult truths.

Six

After my mother died, I phoned my father every Sunday. When Emily was born, I wrote to him every week with news of her development. I sent him photographs of my adorable baby. After a few months of sleep deprivation, the euphoria of giving birth slowly wore off. I began to find it very difficult to cope. I wrote and told my father I was struggling. He wrote me a series of letters in response.

Letter dated 25th December 1993: *"I am writing to you on this Christmas Day having just come from Justine, where she gave me your most acceptable gift. I am keeping very well and am happy to be so lucky as to have the children I have and also to continue to enjoy my good health. I hear from Justine that Emily is making her* *presence heard. A very healthy pastime. I am so glad that you, Gordon and Emily are keeping well and send you all my love - Dad"*

Letter dated 29th December 1993: *"You are quite right about Susan and I, we certainly loved all our Xmas lunches at Ingutsheni, with all Mum's lovely roses to help the festive scene until time, as it does, made them fade away."*

Letter dated 30th January 1994: *"As I sit writing this letter, I am looking at an enlarged photo of my first lovely granddaughter which Justine very kindly arranged to have mounted in a frame given to me by friends at Xmas. She is indeed a beautiful girl and I, you and Gordon must feel very, very proud of her. I am glad to write that I continue to be fortunate in my health and my children. Justine in particular remains a tower of strength to me and helps me manage my life in all sorts of ways, including a welcome invitation to their apartment for a very lovely and most excellent meal. Again, all my love and thank you for giving me such a lovely granddaughter - Dad"*

Letter dated 20th March 1994: *"I thought it would promote your return to good spirits if I sent you a menu from the Sweet Gallery, the restaurant which Justine, Derek and I frequent when I want to give Justine a break from home cooking. I do hope you continue to regain your good spirits and that all goes well with the baby. I keep very well and continue to count my very good fortune in keeping as well as I feel, and as well as my medical check-up reveals I am. I am deeply concerned about the situation in South Africa as our and yours too television coverage [sic] indicates the killing continues. I do hope you continue well. All my love - Dad."*

One rainy Sunday afternoon, in desperation I phoned my father. I told him I had been diagnosed with post-natal depression. I remember listening to my father's heavy nasal breathing on the other end of the phone while I waited for him to say something. "Hell, man, Charlotte, you're not suicidal, are you?" It was Emily's crying in the middle of the night I was struggling to cope with more than anything else. Gordon and I went to see a sleep therapist, who taught us to do 'controlled crying'. This required us to leave her to cry for increasingly long periods of time. The first night I left Emily to cry, I got so agitated after about half an hour I pushed my husband out of the way and picked my baby up. I never did get the hang of letting Emily cry at night. I simply took her to bed with me and Gordon slept in her bedroom. We played musical beds until Emily simply grew out of wanting to be with either of us at night.

Seven

In 1994 Gordon and I went to Cape Town to show Emily off to his sister and various friends. I went to meet my cousin Shelley and, for the first time, I saw a photograph of my Aunt Karin. I noticed that Justine and my aunt bear a strong resemblance to each other.

I visited the Jewish Cemetery in Salt River. There I found Ruby and Mordechai's headstones. My Jewish grandparents lie side by side underneath two enormous monoliths at least eight feet tall.

Letter dated 9th February 1994: *"Of course, I had to return to my job as a young house doctor when my parents died. I was unaware of any of the news you now give me about my parents' burial. No, I had no difficulties with my parents over falling in love with anyone as at that time I was too busy as a student to have time for such frivolities.*

I don't mind your asking me these things one bit. I am delighted with my health and with you, Elaine, Justine and Yael."

The headstones were mainly inscribed in Hebrew. I found someone to translate the inscriptions for me: *"An innocent/pure and honest woman / Ruby the daughter of Avraham / Died in the 57th year / Zayin (9th) Adar Tartzaz – 5697 / May her soul rest in Peace"*

"In memory of our dear father / Mordechai the son of Leib Perelman / Died on tet Vav (15th) Tevet Tarzach – 5698 / In the 62nd Year of his life / Mourned by his children and grandchildren and by the members of the Great Camp of Israel / May his soul rest in Peace"

Shelley explained the Hebrew wording as follows: *"According to the tombstone: Ruby is the daughter of Avraham. That is her Hebrew name. That is how it is written in Hebrew on the tombstone. This is how it is written: Ruby daughter Avraham. It does not include the family name itself. E.g. I don't call you Charlotte, daughter Lionel Perelman. I would call you Charlotte, daughter Lionel."*

At the time I found my grandparents graves, I had no idea my father came from an Orthodox background. He never attended shul. He observed none of the Jewish holidays and followed none of the Jewish dietary laws. Shelley explained my father's situation: *"Lionel's parents emigrated from Jerusalem before he was born. Karin was born in a very religious area of Jerusalem. We are Jewish and it is a law (still observed to this day) that one may not marry out of the faith of Judaism. If a child marries a non-Jew, the parents treat this as a tragedy - in fact the rituals are observed for mourning of the death of a child. This is what happened with your father when he married your mom. He did not reject his parents - his family rejected him."*

I remember my father's sayings: "No news is good news", "Things are bad", and "One must not speak ill of the dead". When I was having friendship problems, he told me "to be sensibly selfish" and to cut myself off from the person who was upsetting me.

My father was twenty-six when he lost both his parents in 1937. Ethel said in her first letter how wonderful he had been to her at the time. She was nine years younger than Lionel, so it was traumatic for her too, being only seventeen at the time. However, in his first letter to me, he said that he felt the demands made on him by his sisters were oppressive and he distanced himself from them.

When I considered my mother's abortion in South Africa, I realised that my Jewish father committed many sins: he committed adultery with a married woman, fathered an illegitimate child and helped his mistress have the pregnancy terminated. According to Jewish law, my father was not only dead, he was also a murderer. No wonder he avoided his sisters and his extended family like the plague. No wonder he turned his back on his Jewish roots.

Such was Lionel's silence over his Jewish identity that neither he nor my mother talked about the Holocaust. I found out about Jewish persecution and concentration camps when I went to see a film called "Sophie's Choice". I was twenty-eight years old. The Holocaust was not on my secondary school history curriculum.

Throughout my childhood, my father's Jewishness was like a mirage in a silent landscape. I experienced it as a maddening mixture of want and wondering. I'd longed to be part of his world but could find nothing eloquent or human to help me; no personal philosophy, no stories, no relatives, no photographs, no reminiscences, no emotional nuances. Books and films of and by Jewish people always make me speculate about his life. I think back to the strangely repetitive tunes he hummed in the car when he drove me to school. I've wondered if these were remnants of things he'd once chanted in the synagogue as a boy. I've wondered whether my Jewish grandparents were in an arranged marriage; Yael said he'd heard that Ruby's head was shaved and that she wore a wig. Was my Jewish grandmother uneducated, submissive, unquestioning? What did Shelley mean when she wrote that Mordechai had given his wife 'a hard time'? My mother's subservience, my father's dogmatic approach to life troubled and frustrated me. I have no memory of my father telling my mother or anyone else in our family that he loved us. I am the only one to whom he wrote letters. I think he did so because my mother was finding my stream of letters and questions annoying, so he picked up his pen to appease her and probably hoped to fob me off.

My father didn't have any memory of his parents' headstones, so perhaps his sisters and the Jewish community in Woodstock had had them erected. The war rescued him from the demands of his sisters, but it got him into hot water when he fell in love with Susan. It's also possible, however, that my mother, being a gentile, offered Lionel an escape from being Jewish. Jews were actively discriminated against in South African society. They were barred from joining various clubs, prevented from working in certain organisations and were on the receiving end of derogatory names; the ones I remember were 'kikes', 'yids', 'shnorras' and 'chaimies'.

When Emily was eighteen months old, Gordon and I flew to Toronto to show my father his first grandchild. By then she was an energetic child with blonde curls and clear blue eyes. She loved nothing better than to stand on a chair and sing her favourite nursery rhymes like a foghorn.

My father beamed at her and Emily beamed back at him.

Part Three

Eight

On 13th August 1995 I got a phone call from Justine to say Derek had found my father lying dead on the bathroom floor at his apartment. The hand-basin was full of water and he was clutching his electric razor.

Justine wrote: *"In the months before Lionel died, you'll probably remember he had become increasingly paranoid about people stealing his blue recycling box and not letting Naomi in to clean - all sorts of other strange things, including not washing well, and slicing and dicing his face when he shaved. I've always thought he knew his behaviour wasn't good, and the road he was on wasn't going to get any better, so he decided the time had come and put the electric razor in the sink knowing it would give him a sufficient jolt to finish him off.*

You'll remember we came to you that Christmas and I think you were a little shocked when we told you our thoughts, but I really do believe he was so scared of dementia / Alzheimers and the fact he was so alone, that he didn't want to carry on. His life wouldn't have got any better, that's for sure. We were always so scared for him and had started to make inquiries into him moving into Baycrest, which is a facility for the elderly who can't manage any longer. I don't think he knew about that, but if he did, he wouldn't have wanted to go there.

During the week before he died, we both were busy setting up the gift show which meant being out near the airport each day, eight to six-ish, so only saw him on the Tuesday night for dinner, knowing we were busy for the weekend at the show. Normally we'd go there, or he'd come here, some time over the weekend. I used to phone him each evening around six, just to chat, but when I phoned on the Friday night, he didn't answer. It wasn't the first time that had happened, so I wasn't concerned. He sometimes just went to bed at odd times. Saturday, I phoned again - still no reply, but we were both at the show, so decided we'd go over there on Sunday when it closed, to make sure he was just being himself. When we were driving close to the building, I could see the lights were on in his flat, so felt relieved that he must be OK. When we got to his door, I told Derek to go because I was scared something had happened, so waited outside the open door. I think I knew he was dead actually. I'd been phoning from the show on and off all day and had told Sue, who also worked at the show, that we were going over there because something was wrong.

Derek shouted to me not to come in. He closed the bathroom door, so I didn't see him, and called 911. Within a few minutes, these huge fire fighters arrived, followed by three policemen. They went into the bathroom but didn't stay long. They told us Lionel was dead and the coroner had been called. After an hour or so, a man who said he was the coroner arrived and told us he'd died but for the life of me, I really can't remember whether he said he'd had a heart attack. I think he did. Have to look at the death certificate to see what it says. [The death certificate does indeed say that Lionel suffered a heart attack]. After a bit Debbie and Bert showed up, as well as an ambulance and the funeral service people, who took Lionel off to their mortuary. It was a long night! By the time we left, I think we were really relieved that he hadn't suffered.

After Mum died, we'd tried everything to get Dad to be friends with someone in their building, but he was so strange that way - always so critical of others and also his neighbour shouted at him about his radio being too loud all the time (remember how deaf he was) so he had no company except when we went over, or he came to us - not that it really seemed to bother him much - he loved his own company always, and enjoyed his radio, T.V and going shopping. He really never seemed dreadfully unhappy. After Mum died, I asked him if he wanted to come and stay for a bit, but he didn't, nor did he cry. He was really such a 'controlled' person - very sad."

Part Three

One evening, like a vision emerging out of a cloud, I saw how cleverly my father had contrived to make his death look like he had suffered a heart attack. He had taken an overdose and had done a great job at disguising it. When I thought about how carefully my parents concealed their suicides, I could see that their medical expertise was a helpful factor. They knew there would be legal implications if Justine or Derek were aware that they were planning to take their own lives.

My father was there when my mother made her farewell phone calls, and when she swallowed her pills. It may explain why he didn't cry in the immediate aftermath of her death. I feel sure that's why suicide was on his mind when I told him I was feeling depressed.

For years after my father's death, Derek joked that if you wanted to get rid of your father-in-law, just buy him an electric razor.

I remember one day Gordon was telling me about some of his father's favourite pastimes and the children asked me what my father's interests had been. I mumbled something about him having a wide knowledge of drugs and a bit of a thing about electrodes.

Nine

Justine posted my father's ashes to me in Oxford, but I couldn't imagine scattering his ashes in the UK. I put them away in the under stairs cupboard until I decided what I was going to do.

On 26th March 1996, I flew to Zimbabwe and took Emily with me. Gordon was in the process of being made redundant and so I went on my own. I flew to Harare to stay with Mel and then I took Emily to meet Yael who was living in Zambia. My plan was to scatter my father's ashes on the top lawn of the big house at Ingutsheni. Yael declined my invitation to come with me for the ceremony. I hired a car and travelled down to Bulawayo where Emily and I checked into the Holiday Inn.

I drove to the hospital the following morning. It was more than twenty years since I had been back, but it seemed like just the other day. I went to the little house first and took a photograph of it. I drove around the back of the hospital, past the women's ward, the laundry and the administrative offices. I went down the cinder track with a rubber hedge on either side, past Donald Brewer's house, past the nurses' home and over the bridge where Yael had fallen headfirst onto the concrete below. I made my way slowly up the driveway to the big house and parked the car next to the ugly concrete dome over the now empty fishpond.

The garden had been swamped by weeds and tall grass, the tennis court was over-grown, and the fishponds were full of rubble. The shelter had no roof and its pillars were surrounded by the remnants of paving stones. The family living in the house invited us in to have a look around. As we took a final walk around the overgrown garden, it struck me how incredibly small the house was. After gazing from the veranda over the tall grasses towards 23rd Avenue, I got in my car and drove back to the hotel.

The next morning, while I decided what I was going to do with Lionel's ashes, I got a packed lunch from the hotel. I drove out to the Matobo Hills. Once more, the route was so familiar it felt as if I had never been away. The landscape hadn't lost any of its power. The roads were bone dry and solid corrugations on the surface made the car, and everything inside it, rattle.

Great granite outcrops loomed into sight as we travelled. Emily fell asleep as I drove along tarred strips and our journey became smoother. Bronze boulders towered over the surrounding golden grassland, balancing precariously on top of each other, their sides streaked by centuries of weather. Torrential rains, lightning strikes, and icy frosts had left black cracks and trails, where transitory rivers had run like hair down their curved surfaces. The car trailed clouds of orange dust behind it and the blue sky stretched above us. We journeyed on past dams, glittering like strips of silver in the countryside. I noticed families having picnics, and others sitting on granite outcrops which stretched into the water like enormous hands. I saw herds of zebra flicking their tails, wildebeest drinking at the water's edge and the outline of a baboon here and there on the rocks. When a giraffe lumbered across the road, I stopped the car and woke Emily so she could watch it as it went on its graceful way.

I brought the car to a halt in the car park at World's View and Emily scampered off ahead of me with her brightly coloured umbrella above her head. By now the midday sun was dazzlingly hot. There was no shade along our path, but Emily's stout legs pumped with easy energy as she ran up the sloping path, along the tops of granite boulders, to the graves of fallen heroes. The sun lit up the great dome of granite which loomed before us. We startled rainbow-coloured lizards out of their sleep. They scattered in all directions, sending tiny showers of stone tinkering down the sloping ground. I heard the 'quare, quare' of a lowrie bird and the 'pee-o pee-o pee-o' of a hornbill.

At the top Emily skipped around looking for lizards. She used her rolled up umbrella to poke them as they lazed around in the shadows of granite boulders, which looked like giant ice cream scoops or fossilised eggs from the beginning of time. Below us stretched valleys dotted with scrubland trees, green shapes filling in the gaps among the rocky outcrops. Swathes of bleached grassland lay before us and shimmered in the heat. A hot wind offered us no relief and the heat rising off the rocks made the air vibrate. The eerie wail of cicadas beating their invisible legs rang in the still air.

World's View filled me with awe and stirred memories of the times I had been there with Yael and my mother.

Emily and I walked over to Rhodes' grave. It looked like a granite wedding cake, with rectangular layers chiselled out of stone. An iron cover with an inscription to Rhodes radiated in the heat. Emily hopped up on top of it and did a little tap dance. The clang of her heels made her squeal with delight. She asked me to read the inscription etched on the cover. "Here lies Cecil John Rhodes", I began, when Emily suddenly pulled sternly on my arm. "Mumma," she said "why did he lie? That's very, very naughty," she said with a serious look on her face and wagged her finger at me. I burst out laughing and couldn't stop. Emily began to giggle and continued with her tap dance. Our laughter echoed out over the hills.

On the drive back from World's View I mulled over what to do with the ashes. Time was running out because I was flying back to England in two days' time.

After a good night's sleep, I decided I would scatter Lionel's ashes at a local beauty spot. So, the next day I drove into town and bought two red roses from a flower seller at the Bulawayo City Hall. Emily sat next to me and clutched the roses as we drove to the Hillside Dams. The black box containing my father's ashes sat on the back seat. There was not a soul in sight when we got to the car park. It was a warm autumnal morning and the water lilies on the dam looked faded and sad. Emily skipped over to a rocky outcrop at the far end of the lower dam. I gave her the plastic bag with Lionel's ashes in it. She danced around on the rocks, scattering all the ashes into the water. Then we walked down to the grassy area alongside the dam and we each threw a red rose as far as we could into the water. I felt nothing but relief; there were no tears.

I drove to Eskimo Hut and bought us each a double scoop of ice cream smothered with shiny chocolate sauce. The following day we flew back to England and I had a strong feeling my mission had been accomplished. Ten days after my visit, I felt extremely unwell and suspected I'd contracted malaria. My GP prescribed anti-depressants. He agreed to do a blood test when I insisted that he do so. He phoned me the next day to confirm that my blood test was positive, and I recovered quickly in hospital with the appropriate medical treatment.

A few months later Yael got in touch to say he and his wife had driven to the Hillside Dams to pay their respects to Lionel. As they gazed into the dam where Emily had scattered his ashes, an enormous water snake surfaced and gave them a fright. Just as mysteriously as it had appeared, it turned and glided away from them, back into the murk of the dam.

A year after my visit to Zimbabwe, my son Tim was born. Like Emily before him, Tim was born at home. I am the only member of my family to have children of my own; Elaine, Justine and Yael are all step-parents. I compensated for my children's lack of cousins by befriending other mothers with similar aged children, their classmates and families in our neighbourhood. Exhaustion caught up with me around the time that Emily turned sixteen. She fell off a horse and I fell apart. I went to see my GP, to ask if I might see a counsellor and that's how my conversations with Sandi began.

Blue Remembered Sky

PART FOUR

Requiem

Largactil on its own has a very high propensity to cause severe akathisia. With the other akathisia culprits, *Zyprexa* and *Faverin* already in my system, a vortex of akathisia despair began to devour me after only a few doses of the new drug. The *Faverin* was increasing my serotonin, the *Zyprexa* and *Lithium* were fighting to supress it. The *Largactil* was subduing my dopamine activity as was the *Zyprexa*.

The *Lithium* also reduced noradrenalin action and caused a general dampening of nerve activity, while the *Epilim* and the *Valium* were increasing another chemical messenger known as GABA.

My brain was a biochemical battle zone.

Rebekah Beddoe

The trouble is that if you are trapped in a situation where you cannot fight and there's nowhere safe to run, you are stuck with your body in alarm mode but not actually doing anything. This leaves you with an awareness of physical symptoms that are uncomfortable and of no use: constipation, a dry mouth, blurred vision, aching muscles, palpitations, shortness of breath. The symptoms might be even worse if your current fears were compounded by night-time dreams or painful daytime memories of past dangers. I found that the Kosovars, just like the soldiers in Gorazde liked these straightforward physiological explanations of their physical symptoms and the reassurance that they were neither imagining things nor crazy.

Lynne Jones

Psychiatry is a massive violation of human rights.

Not a single chemical imbalance has been established for a single so-called "mental illness".

We must protect our children who are now being included.

Bonnie Burstow

Blue Remembered Sky

Part Four

One

One day, about ten years ago, during a meal with friends, I mentioned that I'd grown up in Zimbabwe and that my family had lived at Ingutsheni. One of our friends, Cindy, dropped her fork and stared at me in horror. She said she'd met a woman named Helen who had spent time inside Ingutsheni in the 1970's. Helen was her daughter's teacher when she'd lived in Harare a few years back. Cindy said Helen had told her that her experience in the hospital had been truly horrific. I felt embarrassed and somewhat lost for words. Cindy's husband diplomatically changed the subject. After that incident, I began to look for books about the history of the hospital and found Lynette A. Jackson's study of Ingutsheni. Jackson explored conditions in the wards, hospital records and described treatments that made my blood run cold. The wards were appallingly over-crowded for African patients in particular, and the prejudices against them shocked me. I found my father's name in her book. A day or so after I finished reading Lynette's book, I was woken up by a night terror. I heard a person screaming with such urgency that I was sure someone was being murdered. It was very persistent, so I got out of bed and went downstairs to call the police. As soon as I picked up the phone, I realised I'd been dreaming. I was frightened enough to go to my doctor and ask for counselling. I had six sessions with Sandi in The Talking Space on the National Health Service. Sandi thought it would be helpful for me to talk about my relationship with my father. When I discussed this with Gordon and began to talk about my family background, he became agitated; he felt the past was the past. He didn't like it when I talked about the hospital in front of the children. Sandi suggested that Gordon and I go to Relate. We went to Relate for a year. Eventually I broke down in one of our sessions and said I believed my father had been responsible for the deaths of many people, particularly African patients at Ingutsheni. Our Relate counsellor advised me to seek psychological help on a personal level, so I started having a weekly session with Sandi.

During this difficult and upsetting time, I went to Quaker meetings to find some peace and was approached by a friendly elder. When I told him that I was struggling to write a story about Zimbabwe, he introduced me to Marieke Clarke. I was thrilled to meet Marieke, the author of a book about the pre-colonial history of Zimbabwe that I'd recently bought. As an historian she had heard of the hospital because Guy Clutton-Brock's wife Molly had been given shock treatment there after he was thrown into jail for helping the ethnic majority to draft a constitution for change and political representation. Marieke gave me her email address and said she would be happy to help me if there was anything I wanted to know. She put me in touch with Pathisa Nyathi, a leading cultural historian in Zimbabwe for further advice and clarification as my research developed.

Sandi suggested I see if I could find people who had personal experience of the hospital. I got in touch with Cindy and asked her to link me up with Helen. We met for a drink, and Cindy gave me a manuscript that she and Helen had written jointly, hoping to have her story published one day. Helen's husband had issues with alcohol and had physically abused her and their three children. Helen had been sent to the hospital because she was struggling to cope. Tragically, Helen committed suicide in 2011.

I discovered that Cindy knew Sandi when she lived in Harare, later confirmed by Sandi herself. Sandi's Ethiopian partner works in international development and his work took them to Zimbabwe. Sandi is from Finland, so when I first met her, I didn't think she would have much of a clue about African culture or colonial history. Life has given me some lucky breaks.

Two

"I'm not sure whether I dreamed this or if it's a sort of narrative that was going through my mind as I fell asleep last night," I say to Sandi. "I think I spent the whole night almost falling asleep, and then suddenly waking up with these images and words in my head." Sandi says it's good for me to read what I've written out loud. She says it's an important part of our work together.

"One thing that's a big change is that I'm a girl in this one. After all the dreams where I've been a boy, and even sometimes a curly-haired pet, it's really nice to be myself!" Sandi beams at me and nods her head. I open my notebook and read:

"The umpire announces that I've won. My opponent smashes his tennis racquet against the net post over and over and over again, until there is nothing left of it at all. I go into the clubhouse to find my mother. It feels like I am walking over water. I can't wait to tell her that I have beaten him at last. There she is, sitting at a table, smoking a cigarette and chatting to some of the other mothers. The smoke and her hair are the same colour. She looks up. "You look hot," she says in a matter of fact way and turns back to her friends.

"I won," I say "The match went on for ages ... he had so many match points that I lost count! I don't know how I did it, but I won in the end. He smashed his racquet into smithereens."

"Do you need a drink," my mother asks, looking inside her handbag. "Here you are darling," she says handing me some coins. "Well done love," says one of her friends. My mother blows a smoke ring and I can't see her clearly because of all the smoke. I see my father's bright red face as he walks towards us. He gives my opponent a withering look and says he better 'man up'. He sits down next to my mother and gives me a nod, "Good for you champ". He looks at my mother and says. "Good old Smithy's on TV

tonight, what would we do without him ..." and my mother pours him a whisky. My father toasts an African waiter wearing blue pyjamas. "Good old enigmatic". He smiles at me with his plastic teeth. "Here's to Gordon," he says, slurping on his drink. Suddenly he gets up. He reaches into his pocket and takes out a syringe. I notice that his stethoscope has turned into a pair of electrodes. "Honour thy father and thy mother that thy days may be long upon the land," he hisses at me and I see white spittle in his moustache. He takes another step closer. "One must never speak ill of the dead," my father says with real menace.

*"Don't you dare try to threaten me anymore. I'm sick and tired of this, you know!" I laugh and look up at Sandi. "I was **really** shouting at him! That's why it's hard to know whether I was just dreaming or wishing that I'd been able to stand up to him when he was alive. It's lucky I'm sleeping in the spare room because Gordon would have thought I was really losing my mind altogether." Sandi and I sit together in silence for a while.*

"Oh my god, Sandi I remembered something else. The Baxter's pet name for Penny was 'Dil' – short for 'Dilly'. Imagine that, calling your own child a name like that, when she's growing up inside a lunatic asylum! And then I remembered that Yael's nickname for me is 'Thing'. I emailed him last night and asked him to stop using it because I can't stand it anymore."

Sandi doesn't say anything. Instead she makes as if she's cradling a baby in her arms, rocking it gently from side to side. Later, when she shows me out, she pretends to struggle to turn the key in her front door. When she gets it open, I have a brief sense of release and the freedom that awaits me. I turn away from her and step out onto the pavement. I remember the exhilaration I felt in that moment, like a bird leaving its nest for the first time, an unmistakable sensation of flying into a great unknown, feeling genuinely cherished for being myself.

Part Four

Three

I read up about Rhodesia's history and the history of lunatic asylums. I found material about British colonialism and the liberation struggle which formed the backdrop to my childhood. I read the books that Elaine gave me. Sandi lent me clinical books to help me deal with flashbacks; I was being bombarded by nightmares. When I laid my hand against the cool surface of the wall next to my bed, I felt anchored in the real world, while my head swirled:

> The ordinary native of this country is the dirtiest and laziest specimen of his race I have ever encountered. They have no respect for themselves, no morals, no idea of truth and no sense of shame.... Instead of being raised in the scale by the advent of the Zulus with their good morals and cleanly customs, [they] have dragged the conquering race down to their own level. What they needed was "one simple religion", a straightforward version of Protestant Christianity, which would teach obedience. The influence of the Seventh Day Adventists in a neighbouring district, was 'hopelessly confusing the natives.' There was no need for 'these fancy religions.'
>
> *Terence Ranger quoting Donald Moodie, a Native Commissioner in Zimbabwe in 1899 –*
> *Voices from the Rocks.*

Nkomo visited London in 1952: We went to Westminster Abbey and to the Chapel Royal in Windsor, and walked on the graves of kings ... I began to think about Christianity and power. At home becoming a Christian meant giving up our own old ways to follow white clergymen and a white Christ. Our religion, in which we approached God through our ancestors and the history of our people, was said to be primitive and backward. But here in England, the ancestral tombs in the churches signified the continuity of the nation.

Terence Ranger –
Voices from the Rocks

Drapetomania was a conjectural mental illness that, in 1851, American physician Samuel A. Cartwright hypothesized as the cause of enslaved Africans fleeing captivity. It has since been debunked as pseudoscience, and part of the edifice of scientific racism.

Drapetomania: (Wikipedia)

I read about African customs and beliefs, and gained historical insights:

The posts of a house are held together by three horizontal strands of bark and branches, and these symbolise father, mother and children. The wall of a house as a whole symbolises the mother because she gives warmth (love) to the children. The roof is the husband. It is up to him to protect his family against heat, cold and rain. When we asked why huts are always built round, the Karanga replied by asking whether we had ever seen a human being with corners? An old Karanga added: "You cannot build a house merely so that something is being built. When you build a house, then it is always for a human being to live in." So, a house symbolises the person that lives in it, hence the expression 'the house is the person' (imba munhu).

Herbert Aschwanden – Karanga Mythology

Early whites who visited the monument had problems acknowledging black people as having been responsible for the design and building of such a magnificent construction. They attributed the building of Great Zimbabwe to the Phoenicians. Tributary chiefs sent their subjects to undertake construction work. Granite blocks were obtained by applying fire to the stone and then pouring cold water onto the hot rock. Sudden cooling and contraction caused the rock to split. Rocks so obtained were chiselled into the required rectangular blocks. Rock extraction is done in the early morning when the temperatures are low, or in winter. Certain members of the Mugabe family still carry out the art of rock extraction and chiselling.

Pathisa Nyathi –
Zimbabwe's Cultural Heritage

African cities present a western face, in which the received images of modern popular culture are inevitably evident. And yet, in the face of this influence an important and vital tradition of folk stories manages to survive. These are the tales told by the old people.

Alexander McCall-Smith – Children of Wax:
African Folktales

I came to see that my father's western training in psychiatry and African traditional beliefs were seriously at odds with one another. Lionel's inability to speak African languages made me wonder if he could understand anything about Africans as human beings. The fact that he was a psychiatrist troubled me very deeply indeed.

Four

One day, Yael got in touch to say that a person named Penny Walters had posted a message on his Facebook page, hoping to make contact with me. I immediately knew it was Penny Baxter. Penny and I were incredulous at finding one another 45 years after she'd suddenly moved away. We exchanged many emails and, eventually, I asked her what she knew about her father's death.

She wrote: *"We lived in Ingutsheni for two years during the early 60's while my father completed his psychiatric degree. During his finals, my mother took us kids to Cape Town to visit family. My father was supposed to join us after a week but tragically died during a home experiment with LSD, a very new and exciting drug at the time. He should have had Dr. Montgomery with him during the experiment, but it seemed he never arrived, and my father continued to do the experiment alone. On my mother's return the head nun, Mother Fatima told her about the experiment and said that it was such a pity that my father had not waited for Dr. Montgomery to be present. This is how we knew what had happened. Unfortunately, during my father's years as a medical student, he was always willing to be the guinea pig and have the other students practice on him, so his behaviour was true to his character. This tragic event ended my magical time as a child roaming the huge grounds of Ingutsheni. I always yearned to see you again. We never got a chance to say goodbye and to keep in touch. Thank goodness for Facebook!"*

Penny told me Dr. Montgomery eventually testified that he and Paddy had planned an experiment. The coroner ruled Paddy's death to be "death by misadventure" and so Hazel was able to give her husband a Catholic burial.

When I told a friend of mine how Penny had found me on Facebook, and recounted the circumstances of Paddy's death, she remarked "It sounds like that doctor might have been murdered. Have you ever considered that?" I didn't tell her I had indeed considered it; that I'd imagined my father sneaking next door and murdering Paddy Baxter for having an affair with my mother. I'd also imagined that one of the nurses had been caught stealing drugs by Paddy; that he or she had crept over from the nurses' home and suffocated him in his bed, before putting him in the bath with a plastic bag over his head.

I asked Penny for more details. She said her father was in the process of applying for a job abroad. He gave her a red bicycle for Christmas and then they'd gone to stay with her grandparents in Cape Town to celebrate New Year. Eventually I shared my mother's letter with her. None of her family knew that ether was involved in his experiment, or that he'd been found with a plastic bag over his head. I felt worried that I'd spoiled her fantasy that her father's death was accidental. Prior to the 1970's in the UK, insulin was used to induce a coma in a person who wasn't getting any better. The coma often resulted in an epileptic fit which was thought to have a beneficial effect on the brain. It is probable, given the conditions and the degree of suffering inside the hospital, that at the start of a New Year, Paddy had decided he could not carry on with his chosen profession. chosen profession. My mother's assertion that she'd smelled ether in the Baxter's house may have been a mistake. Nobody can know for sure what the psychiatrists at Ingutsheni were doing among themselves or to their patients; they were a law unto themselves. Whatever Paddy Baxter did that night to render himself unconscious – whether it was an accidental drug overdose, a sexual release that ended in tragedy or an intended suicidal act – remains unclear.

Penny's news about her father's experiments shocked me. It made me think back to an incident that had always mystified me. I must have been about ten because Elaine was there at the time. I'd been hitting a tennis ball against the servants' quarters in the boiling sun and I went into the kitchen to get something to drink out of the fridge. My mother wrote: *"I remember you drinking something, am not sure it was benzene though – why would it have been in the fridge? You took a bottle from the fridge thinking it was water and drank a sip – Elaine grabbed the bottle from you."* Whatever was in the bottle, it certainly wasn't water. Elaine snatched the bottle and said it was full of benzene. I remember the worried look on my mother's face when she asked me how much I'd drunk. There was some talk about me having to go to hospital. It tasted so bitter that I knew I hadn't swallowed any of it. Later, over dinner, I remember my father laughed and told my mother to make sure the servants stopped putting benzene in the fridge. With a sudden shock I realised that the label on the bottle was not 'benzene' but 'Benzodiazepine', the generic name for the tranquilisers which were the new wonder drugs at the time. It could also have been Benzedrine, an amphetamine which was used during the war to keep soldiers alert and fearless. My father served as a Medical Officer in the war and would have been familiar with the use of Benzedrine. Clearly, Paddy Baxter and Dr. Montgomery were not the only doctors who were using drugs. It's likely my father had begun to self-medicate in order to cope with his work, as well as having a young family to raise.

Yael remembered something else. He wrote: *"Do you remember the time Susan forgot to fetch us from a party at the Bulawayo Sports Club? We waited til well after midnight and then decided to walk back to Ingutsheni. It must have taken us about two hours."* My mother was probably taking Valium to help her cope too.

I thought back to my experience of having the measles in 1966. I realised it coincided with Hazel's return to Bulawayo for the inquest into Paddy's death. When she gave my mother the *Pocketful of Proverbs*, not unsurprisingly it had upset me. I realised my father diagnosed my distress as hysteria and gave me a dose of Largactil. I hallucinated and saw miniature green men on my pillow. My father said I had the measles, but I was only ill for one night. The measles would have laid me low for several weeks. My parents didn't attend Paddy's funeral; I guess it took place in South Africa.

I mulled over other diagnoses my father had made. I asked Justine about the time she had her appendix out. She wrote: *"I had my appendix out when I worked at the shop so I suppose I must have been around eighteen. The only other thing I remember was having pneumonia at the little house and having hallucinations of little men like gnomes climbing up my mosquito net, apparently from the high temperature I think but as for measles or chicken pox, don't think so. I did have whooping cough when we lived in England. If I remember more in the middle of the night will let you know."* Justine's memories of having pneumonia and hallucinations seemed to correlate with Yael's diagnosis of pneumonia when he was a baby. It's likely my father gave Justine a dose of Largactil when she'd expressed anxiety about having a new baby in the house. With some alarm, I thought back to my mother's description of Yael's sudden admission to hospital. It's likely my father gave us two younger children a sedative because we weren't sleeping through the night. It's likely he gave me and Yael the same dose, so my brother lost consciousness. I realised, to my horror, my father had very likely sedated us at night for a sustained period of time and that's why I've had nightmares in which I suddenly plunged into oblivion. All my life, I'd woken up with a start, like a diver suddenly surfacing out of no man's land. I realised I'd probably seldom, if ever, experienced a normal night's sleep since I was an infant.

I thought once more of the inmates who worked in our garden and the fugitives that Penny and I saw at the quarry. I started to have nightmares in which I was constantly on the run. I was being pursued by someone who wanted to get rid of me; my dreams evoked an atmosphere of terrible foreboding. During this un-nerving process, pennies began to drop. When my father diagnosed me with appendicitis, I remember telling him I was worried about a school test, that I was anxious about doing an exam without my mother being there to help me. My anxiety had disturbed my sleep, but I have no memory of being in pain. I asked Yael what he remembered about the time my mother and Justine went abroad and left us alone with our father. He wrote: *"When Susan and Justine went to England to visit Elaine, Lionel put us both in the Mater*

Dei! He felt we would be better looked after there than at home. 1969 was a dreadful year for us both – I also had my appendix removed that year and I had jaundice. I was in Standard Five. I was very sick with jaundice in 1969 – I think I caught it from picking my nose and eating what I found! Susan and Lionel moved me into their bedroom for a time, I didn't go to hospital for the jaundice, but I was off school for six weeks possibly longer. I remember trying to walk to the bathroom and falling over. I was delirious for some time and had the most terrible headaches. Not long after I had recovered from jaundice, I started getting stomach pains. Susan took me to the doctor. He stuck his massive hand on my stomach. It hurt like mad, so he said he had better take my appendix out. I was in the Mater Dei for a week or ten days.

Dr Nixon could see the whites of my eyes had started to turn yellow and suspected jaundice when he came to see me. Susan was upset because she had shouted at me and told me to stop being silly. She thought I was play acting because I hated my teacher and didn't want to go to school because I couldn't do my homework. She'd tried to help me do it the night before."

I was shocked at Yael's open assertion that he and I were hospitalised so we would be cared for in our mother's absence. Yael's recollection of our admission to the Mater Dei Hospital was a clear acknowledgement my father had used his influence to get us admitted. I hadn't realised he'd been admitted to the Mater Dei at the same time as me. I wonder what 'illness' my father dreamed up to get Yael admitted to hospital. It seems probable that he put Yael on a dose of Largactil while I was in the hospital to calm his anxiety and help him to sleep. The yellow jaundice that Yael was diagnosed with is a well-known side-effect of prolonged use of Largactil, as too is liver damage. Yael's admission for an appendectomy soon after my mother's return suggests that a further misdiagnosis was made. Clearly, our emotional lives were unknown, under-valued and misinterpreted at the time.

As an adult, Yael has been found to have minor liver damage. He never was addicted to exercise like I was, and his weight gain in later life has become a serious risk for developing diabetes. He's now actively improving his health with regular exercise and a better diet.

Yael wrote: *"After I was so sick with jaundice, I remember Dad took me to McCullough and Bothwell where he bought me my first pair of long trousers and a shiny green tie with a horse's head on it – that was in 1969."*

Justine has looked back at the visit she made to the UK that year with our mother. She had been in a long-term relationship with a boy my parents didn't wish her to marry. When she returned to Bulawayo, he had gone to university. She met Derek a few months later.

I've reflected on how my father often said I was in a 'dwaal'; it's an Afrikaans word which means 'stupor'. I considered the 'benzene' scenario in more detail. I suspect he added a few drops of a tranquiliser to a health tonic my mother gave me to keep my strength up, especially around exam time. I remember how regularly I sipped a spoon of orange-flavoured Vi-Daylin as a pick-me-up, and how lethargic I felt during the long years I lived at the hospital. Perhaps, he believed it would help to calm my nerves. I've recently learned that Largactil syrup was widely used during the 1960's in mental hospitals in the UK, so perhaps this is why it was easy for Lionel to make an association between a health tonic and a syrup which he used to calm people's behaviour on the wards.

These realisations loomed out of a fog. Benzodiazepines, like Valium, were hailed in the 1960's and 1970's as cures for all sorts of mental health conditions, especially for treating depression, anxiety and insomnia. What my father did was not that surprising when I considered how much freedom he had at the hospital.

My father said to each of us at different times in our lives: "You are unrealistic, self-deceptive, deluded, selfish, childish and immature". These are some of the symptoms that psychiatrists use to diagnose psychosis and schizophrenia. My father said this repeatedly about all of us children. Fortunately, we laughed about him and his sayings. Elaine said he was a 'neb – just hot air'. Yael christened him 'the boss'. Justine thought Lionel was 'like a bad penny that just kept coming back'. I called him 'the doom and gloom man' and I prayed that Susan would decide to take us all away with her to live in England.

Trawling through my mother's diaries one day, my attention was drawn to an entry on the 21st February 1980. I discovered something about Derek I'd not known before. Her entry said: *"Justine phoned – Mrs. Williams is sick and maybe dying – at last – so we've agreed to do various last things – poor madwoman."* I wrote and asked Justine about this and learned the 'madwoman' was Derek's mother who had been a long-term inmate at the hospital. In a drunken rage, she had got hold of a carving knife and threatened to kill Derek's sister. The diary entry on the following day noted: *"Mrs. W died in the night – Lionel has done all Derek asked."* Justine said Derek was familiar with the hospital long before he met her. He had roamed the grounds with the superintendent's son who was at Boarding School with him. The two boys met up at the big house and took their pellet guns with them to shoot guinea fowl, while Derek's aunt was visiting his mother.

Part Four

Five

Using Donald Brewer's map and emailing it to Pathisa Nyathi, I learned that the Ingutsheni Lunatic Asylum was built in 1908 by the British colonial administrators of the territory. It was constructed on one of three royal settlements which belonged to the Ndebele King Lobengula. The settlement where the asylum was built was called 'Engutsheni'. The fort on Donald's map was a relic from the king's settlement at Engutsheni. When I was a child, I understood the name 'Ingutsheni' to mean 'place of blankets'. An 'ingubo' was a regiment of the King's protective warriors, a bit like the regulars in the territorial army, who assist citizens with civic duties, and who are called upon in times of need. These warriors wore a particular kind of tribal blanket. The name 'Ingutsheni' was taken from the isiNdebele language and corrupted by the British colonial authorities. When white doctors asked African patients questions like "Where are you?" and "Why have you been sent here?" - they were expecting the inmates to reply that they were at a mental hospital for people suffering from madness (in isiNdebele the word 'inhlanya' means 'mad people' and 'inhlanyeni' means 'place of mad people'). Many replied that they were at the place of King Lobengula's wives. Their words were taken by the psychiatrists as proof they had lost touch with reality and were, insane.

Every Saturday morning my father went to the Nervous Disorders Hospital to give electric convulsant therapy (ECT) to his European patients. When ECT failed to pacify certain patients, an operation called a leucotomy was performed. It involved the use of an ice-pick-like-instrument (a steel leucome) to sever the frontal lobe and thalamus regions of the brain. I discovered Africans were given higher voltage electrical shocks during ECT treatment than white patients, and they were not given adequate anaesthesia. An inmate might receive hundreds of rounds of ECT during his or her time as a patient there.

Many African patients were suffering from malnutrition and other preventable diseases. They earned a pittance working as farm labourers, miners and domestic servants - and food shortages became rife during periodic droughts, which were exacerbated as the Rhodesian War progressed. I learned that at one time in the hospital's history there were over eight hundred patients crammed into wards designed to hold a quarter of that number. They only had four toilets available. Ntete, like many of the African inmates, suffered from the advanced stages of venereal disease. His face was covered in pimples. Venereal disease was rampant in the male ghettos associated with mining industry in Rhodesia. Workers were housed in single-sex dormitories in compounds for African miners only. The facilities were primitive and sanitation was poor. Men spent long periods of time away from their wives and families who were restricted by law to live in so-called Tribal Trust Lands far away from their male partners. Segregation was not only a way of life between black and white people, but between husbands and their wives. The colonial authorities referred to venereal disease, also known as VD, and other diseases like pellagra (associated with poor nutrition) as 'diseases of employment'. The African inmates were made to sleep on concrete floors with only a thin blanket to keep them warm during the winter months. Heavy doses of medication, the effect of shock treatment and leucotomies prevented them from being able to regulate their body temperature normally. It's likely many of the inmates, whose physical ailments were ignored, succumbed to death from hypothermia and medical neglect. I imagine Ntete died of general paralysis of the insane or syphilis of the brain, a serious neurological condition when syphilis is left untreated.

Part Four

It's terrible that people suffering from epilepsy were admitted to a place like Ingutsheni. Epilepsy is not a mental illness. It is a non-communicable metabolic disability. In England, people who suffer from epilepsy have been helped with appropriate medication, to the extent that people with mild forms of it lead active lives. Furthermore, specially trained dogs can sense abnormal electrical activity in the brain, and thus alert their owners who are about to have a seizure. A sufferer can then go and lie down somewhere safe until the seizure has passed.

The notion that a person suffering with epilepsy has been cursed by a wicked spirit is still widely believed in Zimbabwe. Touching foaming saliva or stepping in urine (during a seizure the bladder is released) is considered dangerous because 'ngozi' (an evil spirit) is said to be associated with these excretions. The stigma is particularly onerous for women who fear no one will want to marry them. In Zimbabwe, where the health care infrastructure has collapsed there is only one MRI scanner in the country. Medication is in desperately short supply and so epileptics get injured during seizures, the most common injury being the result of serious burns from falling into fires whilst cooking. Epileptics in Zimbabwe suffer financial hardships through being injured, with subsequent loss of earnings and having to pay for treatment. Epilepsy is also linked to autism and so it's likely many of the inmates at Ingutsheni would today be on the autistic spectrum. Many of the sounds I heard through the hibiscus hedge resembled those made by non-verbal people on the severest end of the autistic spectrum. In African culture, as in England until relatively recently, people with severe neuro-developmental disabilities were shunned and locked away. It is nobody's fault that a child is born with such challenging conditions and their parents need maximum support in order to cope. The fact that powerful drugs and shock treatment were administered to such vulnerable members of society has been an appalling discovery to make. I was also shocked to find out that victims of poliomyelitis, many of them children, were life-long inmates at Ingutsheni.

Alarm bells started to ring when I realised the doctors were conducting experiments. I wondered how Mother Fatima knew about them. My mother once said it was only right and proper that doctors used the inmates as guinea pigs. It gave them a purpose in life, she said. It was good for them to be making a contribution towards medical science and to society in general. I thought about the silent children I'd seen at the St. Francis Home and I wondered what else Mother Fatima knew about drugs and experiments. I wonder how many children died and whether, one day, just as in Ireland, an investigation might reveal the graves of forgotten children in the grounds of the St. Francis Home for Mentally Handicapped Children.

My father viewed artistic expression as a symptom of insanity, all forms of exuberance as a sign of hubris and financial gain as proof of moral rectitude. My being a girl probably added an edge to his irritability but in many ways, Lionel was just as scathing towards Yael. Our father didn't have time for children and that's all there was to it. The more I looked back at my childhood, the more I could see that I had ridiculed myself in the same derisory way he did. I found it hard to differentiate between excitement and fear, between anxiety and curiosity. My parents seemed to think that unless I was in a permanent state of happiness, there was something wrong with me. Perhaps, having escaped the privations of post-war Britain, they considered themselves happy in Rhodesia, where domestic chores were done by servants, and they could afford new cars, fashionable clothing and expensive holidays. For them, life was good but I couldn't help being emotional and a child.

Black people worked in the mines, on farms and in industry, cooked and cleaned for us and looked after the very young and the very old. This allowed us the freedom to lead carefree lives. Some of us amassed huge fortunes. We enjoyed top-class health care, housing, schooling and hospitality at the expense of indigenous people, who had to struggle and fight for equal access to the institutions they helped build for us; with no vote, no right of abode, little financial reward, no sick pay, no pension rights and no concern for their health and safety. Africans and other races were the subject of our jokes. We especially enjoyed making fun of people with learning difficulties, all the funnier if the stupid person was not white.

Six

Black women were considered to be carriers of sexually transmitted diseases and regarded as prostitutes because of the tradition of polygamy as well as the 'lobola' or bride price, originally paid in cattle but under white rule, increasingly paid in cash. They were at a double disadvantage if they didn't learn to speak 'fanakalo' (a mixture of English and either Shona or isiNdebele) because this meant that domestic servant jobs were harder to come by. Indigenous black women were not given an identification document (known as a 'situpa'), which allowed men to live and work in European areas. They were thought backward and hard to educate by their white madams. A woman who ran away from home or an abusive husband, who was picked up by the police or handed over by her family to the authorities was in a precarious position. Many found their way into the hospital simply for being unable to explain themselves in an intelligible way. During the sixteen years I lived there, I only saw the white woman we called "little Miss Nit Wit" out in the hospital grounds. African women inmates significantly outnumbered white female patients, so their suffering was something that I heard but never saw. This has been particularly upsetting and troubling to remember.

The liberation struggle in Zimbabwe began in 1896. The maxim gun enabled white settlers to defeat the first insurrection against the British South Africa Company's administration. I thought back to Colonel Collins and his helpers, Willard and Maxim. I thought back to the ball machine which Maxim man-handled in order to fire balls over the net and I felt a deep sense of outrage. Willard's name too had hidden connotations. Willard is a name associated with a woman who campaigned for emancipation and education; it was also the name of a brand of crisps which were a popular snack. I felt ashamed of Colonel Collins.

When I went back to Zimbabwe to scatter my father's ashes, I took Emily to look around Townsend High School. We called in at the headmistress's office to ask her permission to walk around the grounds. A man knocked on her door while we were talking and immediately recognised me. It was Willard. He had become the tennis coach at my old school.

My mother thought a performance of the African rain dance was a way of praying for rain. When women perform a rain dance, their clapping hands echo the thunderclaps heralding the rain, their drumming feet mimic the rain drumming on the parched earth, and their ululating voices express the relief and joy that rain brings to people through the promise of renewed life. When I went to a Ladysmith Black Mambaso concert during the writing of this book, I was shocked by the realisation I'd seen some of the inmates who worked in our garden performing fragments of traditional dances and songs – that these were broken memories and not symptoms of their 'madness'.

I discovered that the Smith regime used biological weapons on rural populations during the war. Anthrax spores were introduced to wells and rivers, so people and animals contracted anthrax and died. Under the Smith regime the brutal suppression of political activists was regarded as a white prerogative. However, the contamination of rivers and wells, as well as the poisoning of clothing worn by people believed to be sympathetic towards freedom fighters, was a criminal act that I knew nothing about, and this shocked me deeply. In 2008, during a cholera epidemic, many people believed that it was the result of poisoning and not an outbreak of disease. It was difficult to persuade sick people to seek medical treatment from the authorities.

Maximum security prisons like Chikurubi and Khami were holding facilities and places of torture during the war. I read about detention centres called Gonakudzingwa, Sikombela and Wha Wha that were hidden away in remote areas of the country. I discovered there were other doctors who were employed by the Rhodesian government, who regarded Africans with indifference when they needed medical treatment. My father's attitude wasn't an isolated case. The conditions inside Ingutsheni bore an uncanny resemblance to those detention centres, with the additional horror of drugs, shock treatment and leucotomies - treatments my father carried out on people placed under his care. These discoveries were sickening, and I went through one of the darkest times in my life.

African culture has an impressive oral and musical tradition. Africa is a continent which is regarded as the cradle of humanity. I discovered that the Matobo Hills, where Cecil John Rhodes and other white heroes are buried, is a place of great spiritual significance for the indigenous people of Zimbabwe. In terms of importance it is equivalent to the sanctity that Westminster Abbey holds in Britain.

The nomadic herders who once populated the Matobo Hills were dispossessed of their cattle, their way of life and their land, the Matopos becoming a recreational park for the enjoyment of local Europeans and travellers from around the world. My mother used to take me and Yael there for picnics. At the Maleme Dams she steered the Citroen over a narrow causeway to get to the campsite. After we'd eaten our picnic, Yael and I would scramble our way to the top of a kopje of granite boulders, where we sat and looked out over the dam. We spent hours watching fish eagles swoop out over the water hoping for a catch. We would watch the wind sweep patterns on the surface of the dam and shout our names, so our voices echoed back to us over the hills.

Sometimes we visited the Bambata Caves. There I traced my fingers over ancient rock paintings of human figures and wild animals. Evidence suggests that women and children were responsible for making these images while they took shelter and waited for their men to return from hunting. I learned that certain caves in the Matobo Hills are regarded as shrines where people go to consult the ancestors and to perform sacred rituals to do with water and fertility. Ancient rock pools and underground streams flow during the rainy season. People go to the shrines to give thanks for the coming of the rains and their livelihoods.

Cecil John Rhodes was impressed by the discovery of King Mzilikazi's tomb in a cave at Entumbane in the eastern area of the Matobo Hills. Mzilikazi, king of the Ndebele, was placed in a stone chair, and his skeleton was found in an upright position, surveying the beautiful expanse of land over which he ruled. This discovery inspired Cecil John Rhodes to choose the Matobo Hills as his final resting place. He saw himself as Mzilikazi's spiritual equal and the supreme ruler over the British territory named after him. Rhodes even went so far as to have Mzilikazi's skull measured in order to gauge the Ndebele king's brain capacity.

Rhodes' legacy lives on in the United Kingdom. On top of the domed roof of Rhodes House in Oxford sits a bronze replica of the Zimbabwe bird. Stone carvings of the bird were discovered at Great Zimbabwe, a ruined city in the south-eastern hills of the country, near Lake Mutirikwe and the town of Masvingo. Great Zimbabwe was built between the 11th and 15th centuries and at one time was thought to house over 18,000 people. The birds were found in 1889 by a European hunter named Willi Posselt. Posselt found the stone birds arranged around something that resembled an altar. He took the finest specimen despite being told that Great Zimbabwe was a sacred site. He later sold his bird to Cecil Rhodes who mounted it in the library at Groote Schuur, his official residence in Cape Town. Rhodes had wooden replicas of the bird carved to adorn the staircase there.

In 1891 Rhodes commissioned further investigation of the ruins at Great Zimbabwe. This was carried out by James Theodore Bent, who counted eight carvings, six large and two small ones. Bent noted that there were other pedestals missing their statues, so he estimated that other birds had been stolen. Four of the original carvings have now been returned to the Zimbabwean government. They are kept in a museum on the site of Great Zimbabwe, while one bird still remains at Groote Schuur. Rhodes also had replicas of the Zimbabwe bird made to adorn the gates of his house near Cambridge in England.

When I look at the angular bronze bird on top of Rhodes' House, I remember how a symbol of such spiritual importance to Africans was assimilated into the social fabric of my colonial childhood. Plaster replicas of the Zimbabwe bird were placed above the entrance to the administration block and the superintendent's house.

I remember watching fish eagles swooping over the blue water in the Maleme Dam in the Matobo Hills. I remember the twinkling pieces of felspar in the granite boulders around Rhodes Grave and I think of the diamonds that made white men extraordinarily rich. The wealth accumulated from Rhodesia has a legacy that lives on in Oxford and elsewhere in the United Kingdom. There is a statue of Cecil John Rhodes on the front of Oriel College at Oxford University to honour the endowment he made to the college. There were calls for the statue to be removed during the Rhodes Must Fall (RMF) campaign in South Africa in early 2015. Oriel College refused to remove the statue as it risked losing £100m in donor gifts from wealthy alumni. In June 2020, following the death of George Floyd and Black Lives Matter protests around the world, there are renewed calls for the statue of Cecil John Rhodes to be taken down, especially after a statue of the slave trafficker Edward Colston was torn down by an angry crowd of protesters in Bristol. I hope that the statue at Oriel College will be removed out of respect for the indigenous people – men, women and children – at whose expense Rhodes made his fortune. Similarly, I hope that the Zimbabwe bird - sacred symbol of an African nation – is removed from the top of Rhodes House.

Today the Matopos National Park is a world heritage site.

Many people in Britain were encouraged to take up job opportunities in the colonies after the war. The impact of shell shock (now known as Post-Traumatic Stress Disorder) was beginning to be researched. Since the one hundredth anniversary of the First World War women's traumatic war experiences have now become more widely recognised. For my mother, who had experienced the Blitz and the suffering of wounded airmen and civilians in the Burns Unit where she worked, going back to Africa gave her an opportunity to forget about the war. Perhaps my mother shared her war experiences with her many English friends. I'm not convinced that it's wise or possible to obliterate the past. I've found sharing my experiences with Sandi extremely painful but cathartic at the same time.

I wonder if the present government in Zimbabwe knows or cares about the victims at Ingutsheni whose suffering I witnessed as a child.

Seven

Fear was my constant companion when I was a child. Failure felt like a crime and I've feared being abandoned all my life. This was compounded by my strong sense of having been left out of ordinary relationships, not just because Ingutsheni was set apart from society, but also within my family. I recognise now that my mother related more closely to my two English-born sisters. I remember how it pained me one afternoon when I found her playing Spill and Spell with Justine. Their laughter drew me into my parents' bedroom. There I found them sprawled on the bed, gossiping, sipping tea and throwing dice. They often went to the beauty parlour together to have their nails done. My father had no desire to care for young children or other relatives. He grew more attuned to Yael as he got older and they often sat and smoked their cigarettes over a glass of sherry in the evenings. He took no interest in me other than to show his fury at my disobedience to his expectations. That Lionel was Jewish, and a doctor might have made him a compassionate person. He was an Orthodox Jew and he had very little experience of relating to women as equals. He had no reason to apologise to me for anything he said or did to me.

I believe my father's power as a psychiatrist was dangerous because he was accountable to no one. He worked in a self-regulating body of medical professionals. Psychiatry is based on a medical model of human health. Lionel had access to some of the most powerful drugs known to man – and woman. He had the backing of the World Health Organisation and was a member of the esteemed British Medical Association. Lionel's devotion to his profession and to the ruling elite were inseparable from who he became. His prejudices and his diagnoses were hard to distinguish from one another, and his contempt for people struggling with drug addiction, his disdain for 'alkies' and all the other labels he used only served to de-humanise the people placed under his care. Psychiatric training doesn't require personal therapy or counselling. My father's only confidant was my mother. He built up such an aura of expertise about himself that there was no need to reveal whatever feelings of self-doubt he might have had, or the challenges he experienced as a doctor. Here was a man who revelled in the respect given him by his fellows, a person consumed by his many freedoms to do and say what he liked. He had no need to reflect on his beliefs or his behaviour. I believe that the conditions at Ingutsheni were such that he lost sight of his own humanity as well as that of his patients.

I wonder what emotional and psychological support is given to mental health and medical professionals in order for them, in turn, to best support distressed, often learning-disabled and sometimes violent patients? I wonder if cultural differences are explored within psychiatry today? I wonder whose interests are best served by psychiatrists – the medical profession, society, the pharmaceutical industry, the patients or the psychiatrists themselves? The vast majority of people who experience psychiatric treatment don't have the self-awareness or the financial means at the time they are sectioned, to question the authority of psychiatric practitioners or to seek alternative support. Psychiatric patients have little say over the diagnoses and treatment they are given. I wonder if psychiatrists offer any counselling these days? I wonder how well represented black and ethnic minority groups are within the psychiatric profession, and what proportion of psychiatrists are women?

I had occasion to see a psychiatrist twice after Emily was born. I saw a female and a male psychiatrist. Both times, I was asked if I was suicidal, whether I'd harmed my baby, told that I was suffering from post-natal depression and prescribed medication. I took anti-depressants for six months after Emily was born; I was so afraid of becoming numbed and addicted to them that I chopped each pill into quarters. As I began to make friends with other mothers, I felt less distraught about my mother's death. On Emily's first birthday I threw the pills into the rubbish bin.

Families hope a diagnosis of mental illness will give them access to support from other agencies, and it often does. Psychiatrists and doctors prescribe medication because it works to calm people down, and also because social care for young, old and anyone in between, is under-resourced. Talking therapies are regarded as not being scientific enough. For a young person a diagnosis of mental illness can have far reaching consequences. The stigma can have an impact on job prospects, social inclusion and self-esteem. It can burden a person for life. Sadly, too many people in the depths of despair and anguish, decide to end their lives. Suicide and suicidal thoughts are psychiatry's bread and butter; I wonder how many psychiatrists end up committing suicide themselves?

An over-use of prescription drugs can create problems for service users, for government resources and for society in terms of misuse and addiction. Anti-psychotic and tranquilising drugs have many side-effects, some of them serious. Withdrawing from an extended use of a mind-altering drug, or a cocktail of drugs, can be very difficult to cope with. I believe prolonged use of neuroleptic drugs and antidepressants adds to human misery, contributes to the demise of everyday compassion and facilitates the exploitation and abuse of vulnerable people.

Throwing money, drugs and technology into healthcare, without also training, supporting and retaining compassionate humans to care for other humans can end up dehumanising everyone. I believe that electric-convulsant therapy is an assault on the delicate workings of the brain and I wonder if anyone knows or cares what kind of damage it really does. Psycho-surgery and shock treatment cause memory loss so it's extremely unlikely for a victim to comprehend and complain about the damage done. Given the heavy caseloads that psychiatrists have, I wonder how they're able to devote enough time to listen to each of their patients with care and curiosity when we live in a results-driven world? Living a life doesn't proceed in an orderly and measurable way but most social structures suggest that this is how life is lived successfully.

When I became a mother, I realised that diversity is the way of all flesh; there are no ideal children – just noisy, messy, fearful, mischievous, funny, adventurous, needy, curious, innocent, emotional, communicative kids. It's a challenge to give of one's body, mind and heart for the well-being of another person. It is also a great privilege to be in the company of children; to see the world through their eyes, to hear their laughter and their chatter and to share their curiosity about each other and the world.

The challenge of raising a disabled or brain-injured child can't be under-estimated and shouldn't be anyone's sole responsibility. However, because of the isolation and financial pressures, partnerships buckle, and many people are left to care alone for a child with special needs. In previous generations, a mother had the additional disadvantage of having to endure the belief from some quarters that they were being punished by God or cursed by an evil spirit for bearing such a child.

It seems to me the truth is as variable as there are minds to contemplate what it is to be alive on this beautiful blue planet.

It's illogical to locate a mental disorder inside someone's head, when external factors can impact on people and drugs can distort one's ability to think for oneself. It's like taking a fish out of water and blaming it for not being able to swim. It's as if the other fish in the water have decided that there's something irredeemably wrong with not being able to swim exactly like they do. Moreover, if the water itself is contributing to the fish's inability to swim, it's very hard for it to do anything about its situation. The poor old fish will have to struggle mighty hard to swim at all.

The care of a person who can't function independently is lengthy, can be demanding without support, and is often exhausting – something for which my father was fundamentally ill-equipped. Both my parents lacked an extended family who might have given them emotional and moral support. The fact that care, shelter, nutrition and medication are regarded as profitable commodities is a growing reality in the world today. An illness, an accident or having to care for a dependent can catapult a person into a financial, emotional and spiritual crisis. Time spent with the very young, the very old and the very incapable may seem unproductive, but its solace can't be measured or treasured enough and can only be done successfully in the company of others with whom to share its sorrows and its joys.

When I looked at the moral compass of my childhood world, I saw there was no concept of equal rights on any level of that society. I believe that every child has a right to feel safe and to learn about social and emotional literacy in a nurturing and inclusive environment. The line between nurture and indoctrination was blurred to the point of their being indistinguishable from one another in my childhood; finding one's way ought to be a voyage of mutual discovery and encouragement – not dictatorship. A child needs to learn that everyone has a different perception of reality. Being able to share one's reality with others is the essence of being human; understanding oneself as a multi-dimensional person can't be achieved without dialogue, interaction and reflection. We are social beings and crave inclusion in the world at large, more so if we are disabled and painfully so, if we have been discriminated against for no other reason than our gender, skin colour, cultural background, sexual orientation or social status.

Philosophers, theologians and writers of all persuasions are prone to make broad statements about what it means to be a human being. Until very recently in human history, many of them have been white, privately educated, intellectual, professional men. I've asked myself whether their pronouncements can truly reflect humanity, for often they don't include humans whose brains are damaged, or whose brains are too immature or too old to function well enough for them to think, speak and act in their own interests.

Diagnostic language is so commonly accepted in society that more young people than ever before are being given mental health diagnoses and put on medication in order to cope with their difficulties. For many, this definitive and prescriptive language is becoming part of their identity, and this is how they define themselves. Psychiatric language and beliefs about mental illness are so ingrained in the collective imagination that they are rarely challenged and questioned by the general public. A medical model for mental health is upheld by the World Health Organisation and psychiatric diagnoses, treatment and medication colonise the language and approach used to define what it means to be a human being in distress, or whose behaviour doesn't fit 'a norm'.

Dr. Peter Breggin, an American psychiatrist has fought tirelessly to expose psychiatric drug treatments and procedures that harm people. He is currently drawing attention to the NeuroSigma, a device recently approved by the Food and Drug Administration Department which is available on prescription. It delivers mild electrical shocks, usually at night via small pads placed on the frontal lobes of children diagnosed with Attention Deficit Hyperactive Disorder. Breggin suggests that diagnosing children as young as three or four years old with a behavioural disorder, rather than exploring what is happening in their families, friendships, schools and neighbourhoods is a form of mind control. He warns that administering shocks to that area of the brain repeatedly over a prolonged period of time has the potential to cause significant damage, thus affecting the limbic system, and the child's ability to process information accurately.

Psychiatric dogma can be a boon to exhausted, under-resourced, isolated and inexperienced parents, as well as to companies who stand to earn vast profits from manufacturing mind-altering drugs and technological solutions, with little consideration for their long-term side-effects.

PART FIVE

Reality Check

Events do not follow a script. This is being human.

Naoki Higashida – A young man's voice from the silence of autism

Not everybody expects to be comforted. People who have been schooled into never making a fuss or never to "burden" other people with their troubles tend to withdraw when they feel unhappy. They feel safer alone, where they can "lick their own wounds", as the saying goes, to comfort themselves. There are also impersonal ways of getting comfort. A person can find it in drink, eating, smoking, drugs, computer games or other lone activities. These are often repetitive and addictive. Another way of managing distress it to tell oneself: "It doesn't matter"," "it's no big deal", "I don't mind at all". If this is a denial of a person's true feelings, the person may feel calm, but at the price of shutting down a level of ordinary human sensitivity. It is important because it goes against a recent approach to crying babies. Psychology researchers now claim that it is important for babies to learn how to stop crying by themselves [Barry Lester in There's More to Crying than Meets the Ear]. Fortunately, many parents still prefer to comfort their babies. If they didn't, we might find ourselves living in a society of very solitary people, who had learned to control their distress rather than to find strength through sharing it.

Naomi Stadlen

The richest 1% of people in the UK owns the same wealth as 80% of the population, or 53 million people. 14 million people, a fifth of the population live in poverty. 4 million of these are more than 50% below the poverty line and 1.5 million are destitute and unable to afford basic essentials. The five richest families in the UK, according to publicly available data provided by Forbes have a combined wealth of £39.4 billion.

Equalitytrust.org/3 Dec 2019

One of the primary uses of wealth has always been to buy your way out of the common fate, or, at least it has come with a belief that you can disassociate from society at large. And while the rich are often conservative, conservatives more often align with the rich, whatever their economic status. The idea that everything is connected is an affront to conservatives who cherish a macho every-man-for-himself frontier fantasy. Climate change has been a huge insult to them – this science that says what comes out of our cars and chimneys shapes the fate of the world in the long run, and affects crops, sea level, forest fires and so much more. If everything is connected, then the consequences of every choice and act and word have to be examined, which we see as love in action and they see as impingements upon absolute freedom, freedom being another word for absolutely no limits to the pursuit of self-interest.

Rebecca Solnit – What coronavirus can teach us about hope – Guardian 7 April 2020

I've heard many things in the past week and one of the things I've heard is "Well, it's not my problem". So, this is what I have to tell you: If you listen to black music, if you like black culture, if you have black friends, then this is your fight too.

Coco Gauff speaking at a Black Lives Matter protest – 3 June 2020

Part Five

One

I sit quietly while Sandi studies a drawing that I made when I was around thirty-five or so.

"Justine sent it to me this week. It's a nice surprise to see that drawing again after all these years. It's called The Tree of Life." I look away from Sandi for a moment and breathe out slowly. "I've needed to be a solitary sort of undercover agent trawling through all this stuff ... and having to be so goddam careful about asking questions that bring back so many difficult memories. I haven't told Justine or any of the others that I'm writing a book. It's upsetting for all of us. I don't want to hurt them or alienate them. I can't bear the thought of losing my family ..."

"It's such a beautiful picture, Charlie ..." Sandi says.

"I remember when I made it, I wanted it to look as if life was exploding out of that scrambled up trunk with all its inter-twining threads. I was so thrilled to be living in London, and Gordon and I were beginning to talk about starting a family; it's very phallic isn't it?" I laugh. Sandi puts the drawing on top of the wooden cover over her piano, and we sit for a moment in silence. The tree is a vibrant mess of colours. The holographic glitter I used for the stars and galaxies twinkles brightly in the black expanse of space that surrounds it.

"When I look at that drawing, I remember that I was very scared when I sent it to my father for his 80th birthday. You see, he said that only mad people make works of art." I take a deep breath. "I was so afraid that my hunger to be an artist would be a nail in my coffin as far as he was concerned. I honestly thought that the phone would ring, and it would be him telling me that I had finally lost the plot altogether!"

"But that didn't happen did it?" Sandi says with a smile.

"Nothing happened because my father didn't communicate. He relied on my mother to keep him posted about us. Even in his letters, he kept himself to himself." I sigh. "I remember how I used to sit and gaze at your white curtains when I was trying to make sense of my childhood. What really frightened me about Lionel wasn't just his physical violence, it was his certainty that he knew what was wrong with people. He never asked me about anything; he had no curiosity about my perspective on life. He was sure he knew me better than I even knew myself. The really sad thing is that my mother believed in him, and followed his lead. I never felt that either of my parents listened to me, especially when I was upset or worried or cross ... and anyway, my mother was out and about shopping and having tea with her friends so often that Yael and I were looked after by our servants. In many ways, Mary, Margaret and Anderson, and then the guard-boys and Moses and Martha acted like the caring relatives we never had. Being with them in all that sunshine definitely saved my sanity. And ... and I just never could get close to my father. How can you love someone who always pushed you to one side and all your memories about them make you shake with terror?"

Sandi doesn't reply. She sits as she always does, attentive to what I'm saying, with a slightly quizzical look on her face. "I'm so glad that you're not a psychiatrist Sandi because you would never have believed that I was telling you the truth. It would be hard for me to tell a psychiatrist what I've told you because I'd be worried about them getting all hot and bothered and defensive with me. What I found out about the hospital and my father's activities has shaken me up no end. Everyone wants to have a father they can trust, don't they? I was a child for god's sake, so I believed in him and I just wanted him to love me for myself." I sigh, not out of weariness but with a deep sense of sadness. "I've always felt guilty for feeling that an enormous weight had been lifted off my shoulders when Justine phoned to tell me that he'd died. My father terrified me and I just felt so happy that he was finally gone forever ... his disinterest in me as a person was hurtful and I've often wondered why he became a father in the first place ..." Sandi smiles at me and I let out another sigh. *"It's so nice that I don't have to pretend any more that I had a happy childhood. Even though the truth has nearly killed me, strangely I feel more alive and more passionate about life from having told you about what happened. The thing that has helped me most is that I love writing and making these works of art. Do you know, I don't feel worried any more that I'm crazy, it's what I've always wanted to do."*

"You are an artist, Charlie," Sandi says emphatically.

I look over at my drawing on the piano. "Writing and painting, just being creative makes me feel human. It gives me a sense of my own power." I laugh. *"It's kind of proof that I exist and that I've got feelings and a mind of my own. Even though my family appeared to live well on the surface, everything that happened to me was hidden away. I felt like I was just a pest, a nuisance, nothing I did was ever quite good enough. Winning tennis trophies was such a fleeting way of being loved. You know, none of my family came to our wedding ... maybe my parents thought I'd expect them to pay for it!"*

My eyes start to sting. "You know Sandi, when my children were young and I worked in a nursery school, I went on various courses about safeguarding. I would sit there and look back at my own childhood with incredulity. Yael and I were so isolated and alone - our parents didn't care or listen ...." My throat suddenly tightens. *"The worst was when Yael was conscripted. He was only eighteen. My father pulled some strings to get him a desk job in the police. So, I don't think my brother actually killed anyone. I hope to God that he didn't ... you see, so much harm was done ... all that prejudice and indifference ... it's ... it's just so hard ..."*

169

I can't hold back my sobs. Sandi sits quietly; I see her wiping away her tears, and my loneliness lifts in the bliss of feeling fully understood for the first time in my life.

"We are all connected to the soil of where we are born. My heart and soul belong in Africa - the landscape, the spectacular clouds, African folktales and proverbs, the beauty of their music and traditional songs and the warmth of their laughter. There was this enormous gulf of understanding between me and my parents. I am not English or South African. I am myself and nobody else ... I've spent my whole life longing to be anyone but me. I tried so hard to assimilate myself into Gordon's family but I don't belong there ... I belong to no one except myself." I take a deep breath but the tears won't stop.

"It's an uphill struggle ... Gordon didn't offer to read drafts of the book, even when literary agents were interested in reading my manuscript ... maybe he found it too upsetting to see that my father wasn't the man he thought he was or he didn't like thinking about the racist ideology that created the world we grew up in ... Perhaps ... maybe he thinks I'm the one who's insane for questioning my father's sanity ..."

Sandi smiles at me, and I smile back at her through my tears.

There are many perspectives to history because people don't experience life in the same way. Child bearing, nurturing and caring has impoverished and tested far more women than men. Tragically, women have tended to be treated as soft targets in times of crisis, conflict, hardship and uncertainty. History is carried inside each of us; in our bones, our blood, our skin, our hearts and our minds. My siblings and I have been shaped by our past experiences in different ways. Our characters, interests, memories, partnerships and working lives have taken us in different directions. Sharing our childhood history has brought us closer together.

Part Five

To have suffered alone, without a witness to help me articulate what happened to me was horrible; who would believe that I was telling the truth when my father was a doctor? Throughout my life, little things would act as triggers and I would fly into a rage or suffer bouts of utter desolation. Moments of happiness would overwhelm me with anxiety because I was desperate for their continuation. Because I was traumatised at such a young age, processing what happened has been confusing and very frightening.

Epilogue

Towards the end of 2018, I discovered that a new framework for mental health is being developed in the United Kingdom by a consortium of people involved in the helping professions, in collaboration with service users. One of the people developing the new framework is Lucy Johnstone, the lead author with Professor Mary Boyle of the Power, Threat, Meaning Framework (PTMF). Their aim is to change the language used and approach taken to help people who experience mental distress and all the difficulties associated with it. Under the PTM Framework, professionals and their clients examine what a person does in response to an overwhelming situation, rather than diagnosing him or her as having a disorder. Their strategy is to look at what has happened in a person's life, the impact this had, what they did to cope and how they made sense of what happened. In this way, a patient or client becomes an active agent in understanding the strategies he or she developed to cope with or escape from a threatening situation. Defensive strategies can be changed into more creative and life-affirming ones.

People with mental health needs make huge demands on doctors in the UK. Many people choose medicalised solutions for their difficulties or have to go through the psychiatric system in order to gain access to support. I believe that the PTM Framework offers many benefits in helping people find long-term and workable solutions for their emotional and psychological needs. Mental health depends on social support and financial empowerment but what happens if neither social support or an income is available? If I'd sought psychiatric help, I'd have been diagnosed with multiple disorders and prescribed medication to calm my fears and to help me sleep. My experiences of neglect and isolation would have continued to play havoc with my relationships. I hope that, one day, the PTM Framework will gain political recognition as well as the resources and skilled personnel to replace psychiatry's feet of clay.

Completing this book has taken place during the coronavirus pandemic. I'm witnessing people panic buying, worrying about people who fail to heed government advice, and gaping at a world economy in free fall. Perhaps the coronavirus emergency will shine a bright, clear light on the reality of our global inter-connections and frailties. The biodiversity of everything – plants, animals, insects, flora, fish, birds and humans – needs to be respected and understood. Human incursions into the natural world are having major impacts on our global health.

Sadly, given the economic disparities that exist, a minority of extremely wealthy individuals seem to represent the highest ideals for many people, when the truth is, we rely on one another for our food, our clothes, our shelter, our household products, our transport, our sanitation and thus our well-being. Millions of people provide the world with food and basic necessities, a significant proportion of whom live in appalling conditions, working as little more than indentured servants with no basic rights or as small-scale producers with no protection from loss, ill health or disaster. These are the harsh facts of life upon which the world economy relies.

Perhaps people will come to see that insanity is not an inherited genetic disease but a man-made power struggle where dominant ideologies have blocked and stifled our natural inclinations to love and care for one another. We have been persuaded to believe in a world where our ideals, dreams and fantasies raise hopes that exceed our abilities to relate to each other with realistic expectations, and which are pushing the sustainability of our planet to an extreme. Perhaps we will come to see that money means nothing when supply chains simply can't function; that we all matter equally along with our vagaries, that no one is more normal or less normal than anyone else, no one is more or less real. Humans have far more in common than we are made to believe or fear. The coronavirus pandemic is indiscriminate in its impact on each and every one of us, and so it is teaching me to see my humanity, my most basic of instincts, my most simple of needs and my most universal of vulnerabilities.

It is sad, in this climate of fear and uncertainty, to see that human emotions such as alarm, anxiety, sadness, panic, grief, terror - all the ways that humans respond to change and calamity - are being pathologized and labelled as symptoms of mental ill health. How else does one respond to economic ruin, the deaths of millions of people and seismic upheavals in our ways of living?

Big questions remain. Will the insanities of the past continue to transport humanity further and further away from having respect for the diversity of our world? There is already growing evidence that we need to change ourselves and our way of life due to the climate emergency. Will humans learn to respect nature? Will medical science find a vaccine to protect future generations against viruses? Will COVID-19 succeed in making mankind more humble, more accepting of our shared vulnerabilities? How we tackle human suffering – the grief, unemployment, destitution, homelessness, hunger and fear resulting from COVID-19 - will determine how well we emerge from the deprivations inflicted on us. As a species, we rely on each other and our blue planet for our health, our well-being and our security no matter our class, our caste, our tribe, our religion, our political affiliations or our biological differences. Whether sanity, dignity, equality and eco-diversity can prevail in a post-pandemic world is the greatest question facing us and the generations who come after us.

Zimbabwe is in a particularly vulnerable situation. Health and welfare services have been decimated by political corruption and economic turmoil. Ingutsheni Mental Hospital is still operational as are psychiatric units and mental institutions throughout the world.

Acknowledgements

I am grateful to Lynette A. Jackson for her book "Surfacing Up: Psychiatry and Social Order in Colonial Zimbabwe, 1908-1968". My task was made easier by her courageous and detailed research into an under-investigated part of British history. Special thanks to Maggie Hanbury for taking an interest in me and this story over a number of years. Also, to Natalie Young at Cornerstones Literary Agency for valuable editorial help. I'd like to thank my friends, some of whom went out of their way to help me develop as a writer by reading early drafts of this book. A massive thank you to Pathisa Nyathi in Zimbabwe for publishing the first edition. Also, Marieke Faber-Clarke for helping me clarify important historical details, and in the process becoming a much-loved friend. Thanks to my readers for giving me such warm feedback along the way. I wouldn't be where I am without any of you.

Exploring my past has been painful and challenging for me, my partner and our children. I'm grateful to my daughter and my son for helping me focus on love and life as I struggled with my distress and shut myself away for months on end in order to write. I'm indebted to my sisters Elaine and Justine, and my brother Yael for sharing their memories with me, and for their enthusiastic agreement for me to publish this work; also, to Penny Baxter, my friend Mel and Donald Brewer for their helpful contributions.

Many thanks to Marisa Mulgaria and Tatiana Koval at Headington Library in Oxford; also, Jonathan Saunders and Heather Rosser at Writers at Blackwells. My appreciation to David Walshaw, Harriet Lamb, Saskia Osterloff and the production team at New Generation Publishing for your support, patient assistance and attention to detail.

From my earliest childhood, the care and empathy I received from our servants gave me an experience that has sustained me for all these years; without them I might not have known what love felt and sounded like. I wish my mother had defended me against my father but she was on her own in a foreign land and Lionel's power was unassailable.

My mother was not responsible for my father's beliefs or his behaviour; nor am I. Lionel's history is also my history. In knowing what I do, I feel empowered. That I survived him has cost me dear but not as dearly as if I'd been one of his patients. I have my freedom precisely because he was my father and not my psychiatrist.

This book is as much Sandi's as it is mine. The work we have done together has given me back my life. I could not have sustained exploring my past on my own; it has taken me more than ten years to come to terms with what I experienced.

I would not be where I am without my partner's support for over forty years. It's been an incredible journey so far.

Ultimately, I wrote this book for the child that I was, whom I've learned to trust, to respect and to love.

Bibliography of Influential Books and Websites

The work of Nadine Gordimer

The work of Dorothy Rowe

The work of Alice Miller

The work of Janet Frame

The work of Naomi Stadlen

The work of Chaim Ginott

The work of Adele Faber and Elaine Mazlish

The work of Jean Piaget

The work of Gita Sereny

The work of Sigmund Freud

The work of Carl Gustav Jung

The work of George Kelly

The work of Friedrich Froebel

The work of Melanie Klein

The work of Viktor Frankl

The work of Peter and Ginger Breggin

The work of Professor David Healy

The work of Gregory David Roberts

Okay Parenting: A Psychological Handbook for Parents – Mavis Klein

The Female Malady: Women, Madness and English Culture, 1830-1980 – Elaine Showalter

The Boy Who Was Raised as a Dog – What Traumatised Children Can Teach Us About Loss, Love, and Healing - Bruce D. Perry and Maia Szalavitz

Coping with Trauma: Hope through Understanding - Jon G. Allen

Evil: Inside Human Cruelty and Violence – Roy F. Baumeister

Murder: A Psychotherapeutic Investigation - Dr. Ronald Doctor

Anger, Rage and Relationship – Sue Parker Hall

Non-Violent Communication: A Language for Life – Marshall Rosenberg

Getting the Love You Want – Harville Hendrix, Ph.D. and Helen Lakelly Hunt, Ph.D.

Provocations – Soren Kierkegaard

Veronika Decides to Die – Paulo Coehlo

The Chant of Jimmy Blacksmith – Thomas Keneally

True Grit – Charles Portis

Never Let Me Go – Kazuo Ishiguro

Sophie's Choice – William Styron

See Under Love – David Grossman

A Time to Speak – Helen Lewis

To Kill a Mockingbird – Harper Lee

The God of Small Things – Arundhati Roy

Don't Sleep, There are Snakes – Daniel Everett

Unorthodox – Deborah Feldman

Dying for a Cure – Rebekah Beddoe

The Body Remembers – Babette Rothschild

The Body Keeps the Score: Mind, Brain and Body in the Transformation of Trauma - Bessel van der Kolk

Bibliography

Outside the Asylum: A Memoir of War, Disaster and Humanitarian Psychiatry – Lynne Jones

Invisible Women: Exposing Data Bias in a World Designed for Men – Caroline Criado Perez

A Straight-Talking Introduction to Psychiatric Diagnoses – Lucy Johnstone

A Disorder for Everyone – https://www.adisorder4everyone.com (AD4E)

The Hearing Voices Network – https://www.hearing-voices.org

The Voices in my Head – Eleanor Longden, TEDx talk on Youtube.

Drop the Disorder: Challenging the Culture of Psychiatric Diagnosis – Edited by Jo Watson

https://www.madintheuk.com/mission – see also Drop the Disorder Facebook group

Medication-free Treatment in Norway: A Private Hospital Takes Center Stage – MadinAmerica.com

Dr. Bonnie Burstow – MadinAmerica.com, including her talk "Psychiatry and the Business of Madness"

Ruth E. Dixon – Madness Meds on YouTube

Lost Connections – Johann Hari

COVID-19: How we can support each other and ourselves" – Taylor & Francis Online: Journal titled Psychosis: Psychological, Social and Integrative Approaches

https://platfform.org/blog/on-becoming-platfform-an-accumulation-of-catalysts-colliding/

Psychologists for Social Change – www.psychchange.org

For further information about the history of Zimbabwe and Zimbabwean Culture:

The Grass is Singing and African Laughter – Doris Lessing

Surfacing Up: Psychiatry and Social Order in Colonial Zimbabwe, 1908-1968 – Lynette A. Jackson

Malinddizimu: Rhodes Grave - Terence Ranger, with contributions from P. Hubbard, R. Burrett and A. Chennells

Khami – Capital of the Torwa/Butua State - Rob Burrett, Lonke Nyoni and Paul Hubbard

Great Zimbabwe – Spirits, Stones and the Soul of a Nation - Rob S. Burrett and Paul Hubbard

Guy Clutton-Brock: Hero of Zimbabwe – written by his daughter Sally Rosnik

Bulawayo Burning and Voices from the Rocks – Terence Ranger

"Rhodesia had an arsenal of dirty tricks. These included the Rhodesian poisons laboratory, which had perfected techniques for the preparation and distribution of poisoned food and poisoned clothes"- Terence Ranger: Journal of Southern African Studies, Volume 18, No 3, September 1992

The Use of Biological Weapons during the Rhodesian War: (2002) Third World Quarterly, 23:6, 1159-1179 - Ian Martinez

Lozikeyi Dlodlo, Queen of the Ndebele: A very dangerous and intriguing woman – Marieke Faber Clarke and Pathisa Nyathi

Welshman Hadane Mabhena: A Voice for Matabeleland – Marieke Faber Clarke and Pathisa Nyathi

Zimbabwe's Cultural Heritage - Pathisa Nyathi

Further Information

Cradle of the Revolution – Marieke Faber Clarke and Pathisa Nyathi

Prisoners of Rhodesia: Inmates and Detainees in the Struggle 1960-1980 - Munyaradzi B. Munocheseyi

Kalanga Mythology - Herbert Aschwanden

Ndebele Proverbs and Other Sayings - J.N. Pelling

Nervous Conditions - Tsitsi Dangarembga

Children of Wax: African Folktales from Matabeleland - Alexander McCall-Smith

When Hippo was Hairy and When Lion Could Fly – Nick Greaves

Gumiguru - Togara Muzanenhamo

The Rift: A New Africa Breaks Free - Alex Perry

The Boy Next Door – Irene Sabatini

Don't Let's Go to the Dogs Tonight – Alexandra Fuller

When a Crocodile Eats the Sun – Peter Godwin

Rotten Row – Petina Gappah

We Need New Names – Noviolet Bulawayo

Grandma Benches – podcast BBC Sounds – https://www.bbc.co.uk/sounds/play/p08jf6k1

Lightning Source UK Ltd.
Milton Keynes UK
UKHW041827040820
367696UK00002B/97